Language / words

1. Palindromes
2. Anagrams
3. Rhymes and Riddles
4. Think of words ending with "-gry"
5. Oxymorons
6. Words to Fear

Never Odd or Even

Palindromes

A. Tip it.
B. Lager, sir, is regal
C. Lived on decaf—faced no devil!
D. So many dynamos!
E. Yo, banana boy!
F. Dammit, I'm mad!

Anagrams

A. Athletics, lithe acts
B. CONSIDERATE, Care is noted
C. THE EYES, they see
D. GOURMET more gut
E. PROSPERITY is property
F. A SHOPLIFTER has to pilfer
G. A STRIP TEASER spares attire

Rhymes & Riddles

To find a rhyme for silver,
Or any "rhymeless" rhyme
Requires only will, ver
bosity and time. —Stephen Sondheim

Think of words ending with "gry"

Angry and hungry are two of them. There are only three words in the English language. What is the third word? It's something we use every day—look carefully—you've been told what it is.

The answer is: language. It's the third word in the English language.

Oxymorons

(A) Objective journalism
(B) Turn up missing
(C) Express line
(D) Blues Festival

Words to fear

(A) Homilophobia—fear of sermons
(B) Linophobia—fear of string
(C) Rhinophobia—fear of noses
(D) Vestiophobia—fear of clothing

Never Odd or Even:

Palindromes, Anagrams, & Other Tricks Words Can Do

Never Odd or Even:

Palindromes, Anagrams, & Other Tricks Words Can Do

O.V. Michaelsen

Main Street
A division of Sterling Publishing Co., Inc.
New York

Library of Congress Cataloging-in-Publication Data Available

10 9 8 7 6 5 4 3 2 1

Previously published as *Words at Play*
© 1997 by O.V. Michaelsen

This edition published in 2005 by Main Street, a division of Sterling
Publishing Co., Inc.
387 Park Avenue South, New York, NY 10016

Distributed in Canada by Sterling Publishing
c/o Canadian Manda Group, 165 Dufferin Street
Toronto, Ontario, Canada M6K 3H6

Distributed in Great Britain by Chrysalis Books Group PLC
The Chrysalis Building, Bramley Road, London W10 6SP, England
Distributed in Australia by Capricorn Link (Australia) Pty. Ltd.
P.O. Box 704, Windsor, NSW 2756, Australia

Designed by StarGraphics Studio

Manufactured in China

Sterling ISBN 1-4027-2896-4

Contents

Yo de todo te doy.
"I give you a bit of everything."

Riddles & Rhymes

The Best of Rhymes, The Worst of Rhymes

Colorful Rhymes

Although it has been said that there are no rhymes for *purple*, *orange*, and *silver*, there are these.

ORANGE
Blorenge a hill near Abergavenny, Wales
sporange a sac in which spores are produced; sporangium, a
near-rhyme (pronounced "spe-RANJ" or "SPO-ranj")

An anonymous 19th-century poet in a London weekly, *Athenaeum*, 1865, wrote this orange ditty.

> The second James a daughter had,
> Too fine to lick porringer;
> He sought her out a noble lad,
> And gave the Prince of Orange her.

And here's one from Willard Espy's *The Game of Words* (1972).

> The four eng-
> ineers
> wear orange
> brassieres.

SILVER
Wilver first name of Willie Stargell, outfielder for the Pittsburgh
Pirates
chilver a ewe lamb

And here is Stephen Sondheim's solution, first published in *Time* magazine, but also in Willard Espy's *An Almanac of Words at Play* (1975).

To find a rhyme for silver,
Or any "rhymeless" rhyme
Requires only will, ver-
bosity and time.

PURPLE
hirple (British) to walk lamely, limp, or hobble
curple hindquarters, especially of a horse

TRIPARTITE COLOR RHYMES
In this poem by David Morice, WW, May 1993, all three colors
merge into an anecdote about the favorite drink of one of the
Wild West's most colorful figures.

Wyatt Earp'll
Shoot till he's purple,
Then carefully chill ver-
mouth in a silver
Cup, which he'll pour, inj-
ecting an orange.

Other Stubborn Rhymes

VELOCITY
Having once gained the summit,
And managed to cross it, he
Rolls down the side with uncommon velocity.
—*Richard Harris Barham (1788–1845)*

PELICAN
Dixon Lanier Merrit was the author of this familiar limerick.

A wonderful bird is the pelican,
His bill can hold more than his belican.
He can take in his beak
Enough food for a week,
I'm darned if I know how the helican.

Riddles, Relatives, & Dubious Praises

The "-gry" Riddle

Contrary to what many believe, there are only two "common" words that end in "-gry": *angry* and *hungry*. The puzzler Nightowl mentioned the old "-gry" words riddle in her Rochester, New York, newsletter *The Ag Mine*, March 1997: "A local newspaper columnist found the first logical explanation I have seen of that so-called riddle. The correct version of the riddle is 'Think of words ending in '-gry.' *Angry* and *hungry* are two of them. There are only three words in the English language. What is the third word? The word is something we use every day.

"If you have listened carefully, I have already told you what it is.' The answer is *language*, which is the third word in 'the English language.' Most versions of the riddle change the wording and make it insoluble. Let's hope this puts that 'riddle' to rest."

A Genealogical Riddle

This riddle by Mabel Peete appeared in the puzzle column "Odd Knots" in *The Independent*, a New York weekly, Dec. 19, 1894. The theme was later used in the song "I'm My Own Grandpa/Grandma," credited to Dwight Latham and Moe Jaffe, and recorded by many since the 1940s, including Guy Lombardo, Lonzo & Oscar, Homer & Jethro, and Ray Stevens. It was based on a story called "Singular Intermarriages," printed in Charles Bombaugh's *Gleanings* (1870).

> Twas long ago, in the days of witches and the "Bible Laws," that a mysterious old woman took up her abode in a cabin on the outskirts of a New England town. She was regarded with some curiosity and suspicion by her neighbors, and their questions concerning her family elicited such strange replies that she was finally conceived to be a witch, and brought before a magistrate on the charge.
>
> "Who was your mother?" the judge inquired first.

"My daughter-in-law was my mother," the woman replied.

"And your father?"

"My stepson was my father."

"Have you no children?"

"My aunt was my daughter," she answered sadly, "and my only child, but she is long dead."

"And your grandfather?"

"My husband was my grandfather, but he is also dead."

"Well, your grandmother, who was she?"

"Alas," said the woman weeping, "I am my own grandmother and only living relative!"

"Now, by good Mather's shade," cried the exasperated judge, "either thou mockest me or thou art indeed a daughter of the Evil One, and thou shalt burn this day in the public square!" But the old woman said: "I speak only truth, and can explain the mystery if thou wilt but hear me!"

A little later she was dismissed, and the judge was giving to the public her explanation, which he declared to be quite simple and satisfactory.

The woman said: "My mother married the second time a man much her junior—the son of a widower.

"Curiously enough, I later married the widower. My mother then became my daughter-in-law, since she was the wife of my step-son; my step-son became my father, since he was the husband of my mother; I had a daughter, and she was also my aunt, being the sister of my father; my husband was my grandfather, because he was the father of my father; and, as the wife of one's grandfather is one's grandmother, I became, of course, my own grandmother."

Riddled Praises

An 1800s newspaper reported that a clever young writer composed riddles and other puzzles to entertain female admirers. Because they had become expert in guessing the answers, they asked him for a more challenging puzzle. He sent them this.

When you ask a harder question,
To unriddle your suggestion,
I am sure, itself suggests the answer plain,
It has puzzled many sages
Of many lands and ages,
But no doubt you will tackle it in vain.

By taking the first letter of the first line, the second letter of the next, and so on down to the fifth, you will find the word *woman*. The girls deciphered the puzzle and also found, to his surprise and regret, that the letters immediately following them form the word *hussy*.

Chapter 2

When Words Go Awry

The Best of the Worst, Fictive Muses

These excerpts were selected from unsolicited manuscripts sent to a prominent editor of (serious) fiction, who chose to be anonymous. They were recorded in "From the Slush Pile" in *The National Lampoon* in 1981 and 1989.

- "The man wore a charcoal-gray, three-piece suit and sported a diamond ring on his pinky that Sergeant Miller exaggerated to himself as being the size of a hamburger."
- "From the moment he crushed Cora's skull, he knew it was going to be a rotten Monday."
- "Catherine awoke in a panic that she was going blind, then she realized that her eyes were shut tight."
- "Martin knew that under Jeannie's thin veneer of outward convention she was totally naked."
- "He snorted mentally."
- "My day at work had been rather hectic for me, as it had been for the past several days, and I came home exhausted and angry at the world, and at Mr. Whipple in general."
- "Dale was not one to mince words and came directly to the point. 'Hi,' he said."
- "'Os swoh skcirt?' Jack asked when I arrived at the office. 'I'm fine, Jack,' I said, 'But you know I hate it when you talk backwards.'"

Puns & Malapropisms

A *malapropism* is an absurd misuse of a word; a confusion of, or substitution with, a word that is similar in sound. Mistress Malaprop, from whose name the term was coined, is a character in Richard Sheridan's play, *The Rivals* (1775). Here's a famous example uttered by that lady:

> "As headlong as an 'allegory' on the banks of the Nile."

Malapropisms are uttered almost as often as the intended words, and sometimes they are much more interesting.

> A woman applying for a divorce was asked by the clerk whether she wanted the form for "disillusion [dissolution] of marriage."

More malapropisms, puns, and offbeat phrases:

- "Dyslexics of the wolrd, untie!" —*graffito*
- "The cookbook is being compiled. Please submit your favorite recipe and a helpful antidote concerning it." —*Richard Lederer,* Anguished English *(1987)*
- "If people don't want to come, you can't stop them." —*Sol Hurok*
- "Posterity is just around the corner." —*George S. Kaufman*
- "Beauty is only sin deep." —*Saki*
- "The driver swerved to avoid missing the jaywalker." —*Leo Rosten in Joseph Shipley,* Playing with Words *(1960)*
- "Life's a bleach, and then you dry." —*sign in a Chapel Hill, North Carolina, laundromat*
- "Wagner's music is better than it sounds." —*This quote about Wagner is not in the words of Mark Twain, as many believe, though he often quoted it. According to John George and Paul F. Boller, Jr., in* They Never Said It *(1989), the line belongs to American humorist Bill Nye.*

Bill Peterson (1920–1993), Florida State Football Coach, came out with these gems:

- "Pair off in groups of threes."
- "I'm the football coach around here, and don't you remember it!"
- "Line up alphabetically by height." —*(also credited to Casey Stengel)*
- And, after being inducted into the Florida Sports Hall of Fame: "They gave me a standing observation."

Samuel Goldwyn (1879–1974)

The motion picture mogul Samuel Goldwyn was said to have uttered these gems.

* "Withering Heights."
* "Tell me, how did you love the picture?"
* "We have all passed a lot of water since then." He intended to say: "A lot of water has passed under the bridge."
* "No, thanks; coffee isn't my cup of tea."

On the subject of color television:

* "I won't believe it until I see it in black and white."
* "When I want your opinion, I'll give it to you."
* "We're overpaying him, but he's worth it."
* "I had a monumental idea last night, but I didn't like it."
* "I never put on a pair of shoes until I've worn them for five years."
* "I never liked you, and I always will."
* "I may not always be right, but I'm never wrong."
* "For your information, I would like to ask you a question."
* "Going to call him William? What kind of name is that? Every Tom, Dick, and Harry's called William. Why don't you call him Bill?"
* "Let's have some new clichés."
* "The scene is dull. Tell him to put more life into his dying."
* "If I could drop dead right now, I'd be the happiest man alive."

. . . And Not Goldwyn

According to *They Never Said It*, Samuel Goldwyn never said these lines:

* "Include me out."
* "I read part of it all the way through."
* "Our comedies are not to be laughed at."
* "An oral contract isn't worth the paper it's written on." —What he actually said was: "His verbal contract is worth more than the paper it's written on," referring to film executive Joseph M. Schenk.

And Goldwyn denied having said:

> "Anyone who goes to a psychiatrist ought to have his head examined!"

Yogi Berra (1925–)

These Yogi Berra jewels come from Phil Pepe's *The Wit & Wisdom of Yogi Berra* (1974), among other sources:

- On the shadows cast on Yankee Stadium's left field in the fall: "It gets late early out there."
- To a friend, while working as a head waiter at a St. Louis restaurant: "Nobody comes to this restaurant—it's always too crowded."
- Referring to Yankees manager Miller Huggins: "If Miller was alive today, he'd be turning over in his grave."
- When asked about his disputes with Yankees owner George Steinbrenner: "Oh, George is all right—we just agree different."
- About baseball: "Baseball is ninety percent mental. The other half is physical."
- On being quoted: "I really didn't say everything I said."
- Dale Berra, when asked to compare himself to his father: "Our similarities are different."

Famous Fumbles & Witty Quotes

- "The climate of the Sahara is such that its inhabitants have to live elsewhere." —*Antony Lake in Joseph Shipley's* Playing with Words *(1960)*
- "All I want out of you is silence, and damn little of that!" —*a judge in Joseph Shipley's* Playing with Words *(1960)*
- "A lot of people my age are dead at the present time." —*Casey Stengel*
- "You should go to your friend's funeral; otherwise, he might not come to yours." —*Anonymous*
- During a trial in Salisbury, Rhodesia (now Zimbabwe), a witness was asked if the accused was conscious or unconscious at the scene of the crime. "He was pretending to be conscious, but he wasn't," replied the witness.

Mondegreens (Aural Malapropisms)

A *mondegreen* is an aural malapropism—a mishearing of a word or phrase. The term was coined by writer Sylvia Wright. A word or phrase which sounds the same as another has been referred to as an *oronym*, similar to a charade or *redivider*. Columnist Jon Carroll of the *San Francisco Chronicle* explains that Wright had heard the Scottish ballad "The Bonny Earl of Murray" as a child and thought one stanza read like this.

> Ye highlands and ye lowlands
> Oh, where have you been?
> Thou have slay the Earl of Murray
> And Lady Mondegreen.

"Poor Lady Mondegreen, thought Sylvia Wright—a tragic heroine dying with her liege. How poetic. When she learned years later that what they had actually done was slay the Earl of Murray and 'laid him on the green,' Wright was so distraught by the sudden disappearance of her heroine that she memorialized her with the neologism."

Something to Sing About

Jon Carroll also supplied these mishearings of song lyrics. Of course, with wine and song, words easily run into each other.

- "We risked our lives in traffic." ("We tripped the light fantastic," from "Sidewalks of New York.")
- "Midnight after you're wasted . . ." ("Midnight at the Oasis")
- "There's a bathroom on the right." ("There's a bad moon on the rise," from "Bad Moon Rising.")
- "The girl with colitis goes by." ("The girl with kaleidoscope eyes," from the Beatles' "Lucy in the Sky with Diamonds.")

From an anonymous "mis-hearer:"

- "Who robbed the milk cow now?" ("Who wrote the Book of Love," from the Four Seasons' "The Book of Love")
- "Hey, you, get off 'a my plow. . ." ("Get Off Of My Cloud" by The Rolling Stones)

A Political Smear

In 1950, it was reported that Congressman George Smathers defeated incumbent Senator Claude Pepper in the Florida Democratic Senatorial Primary by circulating, in rural communities of northern Florida, literature stating that the senator, a known "extrovert," had "matriculated" with young women. Smathers also accused Pepper's sister of being a "thespian" and his brother of being a "practicing 'homo sapiens.'" As if that wasn't enough, Smathers used McCarthyism as leverage against his opponent by referring to him as the "Red" Pepper.

Silver Spoonerisms

A *spoonerism* is an unintentional (usually) transposition of letters or syllables in words.

The term *spoonerism* was named after the Reverend William Archibald Spooner, warden of New College in Oxford, England, from 1903 to 1924, holder of the first honorary degree in *orthinology*—or "word botching."

Before Spooner, this form of metathesis was sometimes called a "marrowsky," after a Polish count who supposedly suffered from the disorder. These, like malapropisms, can often be more interesting than the intended phrase. The following spoonerisms were attributed to the clergyman, though few, if any, were actually uttered by him:

- To a woman in church: "Mardan me, padom, but you are occupewing my pie. Allow me to sew you to another sheet."
- To one of his students: "You have hissed my mystery classes; you have tasted two worms!"
- To a group of farmers: "I have never addressed so many 'tons of soil.'"
- "I have in my bosom a half-warmed fish" (half-formed wish).
- To a bridegroom: "It is kisstomary to cuss the bride."
- "He is a 'newted nose' analyst."
- "His sin twister."
- "Is the bean dizzy?"
- "Our 'queer old Dean'" (dear old Queen [Victoria]).

More Spoonerisms

- "A waist is a terrible thing to mind."
- "Now missen, lister, all I had was tree marthroonis. So I theem under the affluence of inkahol, I am not palf as hickled as thinkle peep I am." —*Martin Gardner, O&C (1961)*
- "I'd rather have a (free) bottle in front o' me than a (pre)frontal lobotomy." —*source uncertain; attributed to William Faulkner, 1949; also credited to both Dorothy Parker and Fred Allen*
- "You can't book a judge by his cover."
- "A drama critic is a man who leaves no turn unstoned." —*George Bernard Shaw*
- "It's tired and I'm getting late." —*from the 1960s Peter Rowan song "Home to You"*
- "I remember your name, but I just can't think of your face."
- "Time wounds all heels." —*Groucho Marx*
- "I am a conscientious man./When I throw rocks at birds/ I leave no tern unstoned./I am a meticulous man/and when I portray baboons/I leave no stern untoned." —*Ogden Nash*
- On a graffiti wall, an anonymous philosopher penned: "I am, therefore I think," And was answered with: "Aren't you putting Descartes before the horse?"
- George S. Kaufman's response to his daughter after she told him that a friend of hers from college had eloped: "Ah! She put her heart before the course!"
- Historical reminder: "Always put Horace before Descartes." —*Donald O. Rickter*
- A documented example is this gem by a newscaster: "Rumor that the President would veto the bill came from a high 'White Horse souse.'" (The White Horse is a famous New York tavern where Dylan Thomas is said to have drunk himself to death.) —*Kermit Schafer's "Pardon My Blooper," an audio collection of broadcast blunders.*
- In 1960, while campaigning in St. Paul, Minnesota, Adlai Stevenson was offended by a political remark made by clergyman Norman Vincent Peale. When questioned by the press about his visit, Stevenson said he found St. Paul "appealing" and Peale "appalling." —*Martin Gardner, Scientific American, Sept. 1964*

Spoonerhymes & Spoonergrams

DOUBLE SPOONS

Here is a spoonerhyme by K. F. Ross, from the *Mensa Bulletin*, Apr. 1969.

> Ill wit.
> Will it
> Die out?
> I doubt.

SYLVAN SPRING

Alfred Kohn's poem "Sylvan Spring," from Willard Espy's *The Word's Gotten Out* (1989), contains spoonerhymes and near-spoonerhymes.

> The snowdrops push through soggy grounds;
> The she-bear senses spring is here.
> Her mate still mumbles groggy sounds;
> She wheezes softly in his ear.
> Outside the den, a doe and fawn
> Are hiding from their foe at dawn.
> Amid bare trees a dreary lake
> Is harboring a leery drake.
> Two robins gather reed for nest,
> And later they have need for rest.
> A frog is eyeing a blue fly.
> (It missed the one that just flew by.)
> A chipmunk, furried little ball,
> Digs nuts it buried in the fall.
> So there are creatures, weak and mild,
> And others meek, and others wild.

The Power of Poor Translations

Slogans Abroad

Executives of Coca-Cola were puzzled as to why sales of their product were doing poorly in mainland China until they discovered that the Chinese symbols CO CA CO LA were erroneously translated as "bite the wax tadpole," or "female horse stuffed with wax."

The Chinese translation of the Kentucky Fried Chicken slogan "finger-licking good" was given as "eat your fingers off."

In Taiwan, the Pepsi-Cola Company was told that its slogan, "Come Alive with the Pepsi Generation," was translated as "Pepsi brings back your dead ancestors."

Electrolux, a Scandinavian vacuum-cleaner manufacturer, advertised its product in the United States with the slogan: "Nothing sucks like an Electrolux."

Batman was a movie box-office hit in 1989 in the United States, but it did not fare so well in Scandinavia. Perhaps one reason was the difficulty in translating the title. In Norway, for instance, it appeared on theater marquees as *Flaggermous Man* ("Flying Mouse Man").

According to actor-comedian Billy Crystal, in France the title of the film *City Slickers* (1991), in which he co-starred, was changed to *Life, Love & Cows.* (There is no French word equivalent to *slickers.*)

General Motors found to its embarrassment that, in Spanish, Nova (*"no va"*) means "It won't go."

From the Menu

In honor of the visiting Pope John Paul II, a hotel in Wroclaw, Poland, printed a special menu in three languages—Polish, German, and English. The English menu contained:

- Limp red beet soup with cheesy dumplings in the form of a finger
- Sirloin in clotted cream
- A slice of bovine meat
- Beef rashers, beaten up in the country people fashion
- Ham below the knee, pickled and cooked
- Roasted duck let loose

Other offerings that have been noted:

- Europe—garlic coffee with sweat from the trolley
- Vietnam—pork with fresh garbage
- Bali—toes with butter and jam
- Spain—goose barnacles
- China—cold shredded children and sea blubber in spicy sauce

Japanglish T.V.

Here are some English translations of actual Japanese television programs, as listed in *Japan Times*.

- "Babbling Music Hall"
- "Welfare Sumo"
- "Quiz Time Shock"
- "Music Tomato Japan"
- "Young Oh Oh"
- "It's Laughing"
- "Joyful Map Variety"
- "Unknown World: 'Toilet Seats of the World'"
- Special: "Naked Clans of the World"
- "Surprise World #1: 'Fried Ants'"

British Broadcast Blunders

Here is a selection of "Outtakes of the Year" found in a series of London's *Listener* magazine:

- "Clearly the Prime Minister's devious hand is afoot." —*John Smith, referring to a cabinet reshuffle; "The World Tonight" (Radio 4)*
- "The reason he is struggling to bowl straight is because his head is in the wrong place." —*Fred Trueman, referring to Greg Thomas, "Test Match Special" (Radio 3)*
- "I'll come back to the free interchange of needles for drug addicts if anyone's interested in pushing that point." —*Raymond Kendal, secretary-general of Interpol, "Call Nick Ross" (Radio 4)*
- "Most dreams are about everyday things—falling, flying, walking naked down the street." —*Russ Parker, "Dreaming" (Radio 4)*
- "They'd spent the weekend in a ditch waiting for a duck to fly over with a shotgun." —*Peter Benson, novelist, "Kaleidoscope" (Radio 4)*
- "The chief dietician at Crew Hospital had only a skeleton staff." —*"The Food Program" (Radio 4)*
- "The banks have to watch their backs on that front." —*"The Financial World Tonight" (Radio 4), Oct. 1990*

Unusual Names & Titles

In matters of naming people, places, and things, we seem to have infinite resources. We tolerate and even celebrate the bizarre, unusual, suggestive, and uncannily appropriate.

True Individuals

Constant Agony—former resident of Chazy Lake, New York

Itis Akin—former resident of Atlanta, Georgia

Dr. Bonebrake—(there are several, including a dentist and a chiropractor)

Dr. Carver—surgeon in Bartlesville, Oklahoma

Dr. Cheek—facial cosmetic surgeon in Jackson, Mississippi

Col. Clarence Clapsaddle—U.S. Army (West Point, class of 1940)

Genghis Cohen—Orewa, New Zealand

Groaner Digger—Houston undertaker

G. Zippidy Duda—North Atlanta, Georgia

Bob Dunker—lifeguard from Capitola, California, known for heroism

Lotta Dust—a tombstone in Roselawn Cemetery, Detroit, Michigan, reads: "Here lies Lotta Dust"

Dr. Hatchet—surgeon in Bartlesville, Oklahoma

Ima Hogg—of Houston, daughter of Texas governor; Ura Hogg is apocryphal

Judge Law and **Judge Judge**—dispensed justice in Santa Ana, California

Mayor Lawless—Port Lucie, Florida

Captain Mariner Rosemary Mariner—officer in the U.S. Navy

Katz Meow—former resident of Hoquiam, Washington

Noyes—"no" "yes" might well succeed as a politician

Judge Outlaw

Warren Peace—there are many

Purvy Purviance—former executive director, Crime Stoppers International

I. C. Shivers—of John Hancock Life Insurance Company

Cardinal Sin—archbishop of Manila, Philippines

Chip Splinter—cosmetic surgeon in La Mesa, California

A. Swindler—Xenia, Ohio, and many other locales

William L. Toothaker—dentist in Pomona, California

Justin Tune—chorister, class of 1947, Princeton, New Jersey

Original Names of Famous People

Famous Name	Original Name
Albert Brooks	Albert Einstein
Michael Caine	Maurice Joseph Mickelwhite
Tom Cruise	Thomas Cruise Mapother IV
Bobby Darin	Walden Robert Cassotto
John Denver	Henry John Deutschendorf, Jr.
Stewart Granger	James Stewart
Jay Leno	James Douglas Muir Leno
Loretta Lynn	Loretta Webb
Michael Keaton	Michael Douglas
Lorrie Morgan	Loretta Lynn Morgan
Hugh O'Brian	Hugh Krampe
Roy Rogers	Leonard Slye
"Jersey" Joe Walcott	Arnold Raymond Cream
Jerry Jeff Walker	Ronald Crosby
John Wayne	Marion Michael Morrison
Stevie Wonder	Steveland Judkins Morris
Tammy Wynette	Virginia Wynette Pugh

Howard Be Thy Name?

The birth name of novelist Anne Rice (1941–) was Howard Allen O'Brien. Her mother named the child after her father. On her first day of school, the girl introduced herself as "Anne" and decided to keep the name.

Major-league baseball has had its share of interesting names:

- Ty Pickup
- Tony Suck
- Shadow Pyle
- Clay Touchstone
- Urban Shocker
- Van Lingle Mungo

Matchmaker, Matchmaker. . . just suppose:

- Swoosie Kurtz married Patrick Swayze . . . —*Wanta Shelton*, WF
- Tuesday Weld married Fredric March II . . .
- Alison Eastwood married Stevie Wonder, then married Edwin Land . . . —*Richard Lederer*, WF

No Longer at Large

"A Mr. Death named his sons Jolly and Sudden; A man named Sykes named his sons Lovewell, Dowell, Diewell, and Farewell." —*William Walsh*, Handy-Book *(1892)*

Quite an Establishment

Curl Up & Dye—beauty salon, New Berlin, Wisconsin
Hannah & Her Scissors—beauty salon in Miami Beach, Florida
French Liquors—spirit shop, French Lick, Indiana
Nukem—now-defunct producer of fuel for atomic parts in the former West Germany
The Grill from Ipanema—Brazilian restaurant in Washington, D.C.

Put You in Your Place

These place names, it would seem, variously comment on character, place, or an event that occurred in that location. In a few cases, it is the result of a coincidental but amusing transposition from another language.

- Action—North Carolina; Oregon
- Bland—Florida; Missouri; New Mexico; Virginia; NSW, Australia
- Boring—Oregon; Denmark
- Coward—South Carolina
- Dick—Michigan
- Eros—Louisiana
- French Lick—Indiana
- Given—West Virginia
- Hell—Michigan; Cayman Islands; Netherlands; Norway
- Imposible—Mexico
- Joe Batt's Arm—Newfoundland
- Kindred—North Dakota
- Love—Illinois; Kentucky; Mississippi; Virginia
- Money—Mississippi
- Nuttsville—Virginia
- Odd—West Virginia
- Peculiar—Missouri
- Quality—California; Georgia; Kentucky
- Rapture—Indiana
- Silly—Belgium
- Spread Eagle—Wisconsin
- Stab—Kentucky
- Sucker—Idaho
- Tallyho—Pennsylvania; West Virginia
- Uniform—Alabama
- Unique—Iowa
- Virtue—Tennessee
- Why—Arizona
- Xenophon—Tennessee
- Youth—Georgia
- Zephyr—North Carolina

The Street Where You Live

You'll find Nameless Road, in Nameless Valley in Williamson County near Austin, Texas.

North Street, in Ventura, California, runs east and west, so it is possible to walk east on the south side of West North Street. —*Ken Elrod*, WF

A North Street that runs east and west can also be found in Lima, Ohio . . . along with a West Street that runs north and south. North Street is, of course, divided into East North Street and West North Street; while West Street is divided into North West Street and South West Street. It only gets confusing when West North Street and North West Street intersect . . . but residents seem unfazed. —*Julia Strawn*, WF

North, West, and East streets run north and south in Jackson, Mississippi, but South street runs east and west. South intersects South West, but North runs out before it can cross South. East is southwest of South, West, and North. —*Mark Johnson*, WF

What's In a Name?

French King Charles the Mad (VI) was formerly known as Charles the Well Beloved.

Before Stephen Foster decided to title his song "Old Folks at Home," he considered calling it "Way Down Upon the Yazoo River" or "Way Down Upon the Pee Dee River."

In Feb. 1986, a county in Washington state was changed from King, for former U.S. Vice President William Rufus de Vane King, under Franklin Pierce, to King, for Martin Luther King, Jr.

In Jan. 1992, David Powers entered the race for Governor of Washington state as Nobody.

In the 1979 Louisiana gubernatorial election, Luther Knox— dissatisfied with the mainstream choice of candidates offered to voters—entered the race under his legally changed name: None of the Above.

Despite his devotion to the cause, he never made it to the ballot.

Texan Gary Eugene Duda had his middle name legally changed to Zippidy and now answers to G. Zippidy Duda. —*Ken Elrod*, WF

A Mrs. Dorsey, who had been widowed for several years, decided to have the name on her bank card changed from (the late) Mr. Dorsey to Mrs. Dorsey. On the form, in the space "husband's name," she wrote "deceased." Two weeks later, the card arrived in the mail addressed to Mr. Deceased.

Rock stars Grace Slick and Paul Kantner named their daughter god, using a lower-case "g," for modesty. They renamed her China, with a capital "C."

Peter Eastman, Jr., of Carpinteria, California, at the age of 17 had his name legally changed to Trout Fishing in America, as a tribute to the 1967 book by Richard Brautigan.

Boxer Marvin Hagler had his name legally changed to Marvelous Marvin Hagler.

Patrick Allen, a white-bearded gentleman of Harrisburg, Pennsylvania, had his name legally changed to Santa A. Clause.

A lacertiliaphile had his name legally changed to Henry Lizardlover.

Until 1796, the state of Tennessee was named Franklin, after Benjamin Franklin.

Before 1847, San Francisco was called Yerba Buena.

Regina, capital of the province of Saskatchewan, Canada, was named Pile O'Bones until 1882.

In the name Harry S. Truman, the period after the "S" is optional.

A resident of Tangier, Morocco, is called a Tangerine.

Is it a mere coincidence that the letters in Hal, the name given to the computer in the film *2001: A Space Odyssey* (1968), are the letters of the alphabet that precede I-B-M? The director of the film claimed that the name was a hybrid of the two principal learning systems, Heuristic and Algorithmic.

Books & Authors

Pen Names of Famous Authors

- English poet Robert Southey also signed himself Abel Shufflebottom.
- Geoffrey Crayon was one of at least three pseudonyms used by Washington Irving.
- William Makepeace Thackeray was also known as Michael Angelo Titmarsh.

Odd Book Titles & Aptly Named Authors

Russell Ash and Brian Lake collected these:

Odd Book Titles
- *New Guinea Tapeworms & Jewish Grandmothers* (1981) by Robert S. Desowitz
- *Favorite Flies & Their Histories* (1955) by Mary Orvis Marbury
- *How to Cook Husbands* (1899) by Elizabeth Strong Worthington

Aptly Named Authors in Bizarre Books
- *Art of Editing* (1982) by Jack Sissors and Floyd Baskette
- *Diseases of the Nervous System* (1933) by Baron Brain
- *Motorcycling for Beginners* (1980) by Geoff Carless
- *Land Speed Record* (1971) by Cyril Posthumus
- *Running Duck* (1979) by Paula Gosling

Country Song Titles

- "You're the Hangnail in My Life . . . . and I can't bite you off"
- "My Uncle Used to Love Me, but She Died"
- "Not Tonight, I've Got a Heartache"
- "You Can't Get Love from an Artificial Heart"
- "She Got the Gold Mine, I Got the Shaft"
- "Heaven's Just a Sin Away"
- "If You're Going to Do Me Wrong, Do It Right"
- "I Don't Know Whether to Kill Myself or Go Bowling"
- "Where Were You When the Ship Hit the Sand?"
- "Thanks to the Cat House, I'm in the Dog House with You"
- "I Meant Every Word That He Said"
- "I Still Miss You, Baby, but My Aim's Gettin' Better"
- "If the Jukebox Took Teardrops, I'd Cry All Night Long"
- "Been Roped and Thrown by Jesus in the Holy Ghost Corral"
- "Thank God and Greyhound (You're Gone)"

Proposed Song Titles

These would-be song titles appeared in the "Wordplay" column of the *Mensa Bulletin*, Nov. 1987:

- "I've Got a Strong Right to Love You with a Week Left to Live" —*Wayne Silka*
- "I'm a Rabbit in the Headlights of Your Love" —*Chris Hunt*

Ludicrous Acronyms

BANANA—Build Absolutely Nothing Anywhere Near Anybody. *A relative of NIMBY—Not In My Back Yard.*

CINCUS—Commander-In-Chief, U.S. fleet. Coined by the Navy during World War II, but dropped after the attack on Pearl Harbor.

CREEP Committee to Re-Elect the President (Richard Nixon). *A fund-raising organization run by many government officials later convicted for involvement in Watergate.*

DAM—Mothers Against Dyslexia. *Attributed to comedian and actor Max Alexander.*

FOE—Females Opposed to Equality.

FRUMPIE—Formerly Radical Upwardly Mobile Professional. *Coined by California Assemblyman Tom Hayden.*

G.O.D.—Guaranteed Overnight Delivery. *This New Jersey trucking firm's telephone is 1-800-DIAL GOD.*

MUFFIE—Middle-aged Urban Failure.

OINK—One Income, No Kids.

PAL—Prisoner At Large.

PEEK—People for the Enjoyment of Eyeballing Knees. *A 1970s group opposing below-the-knee skirts.*

SAHAND—Society Against "Have A Nice Day."

SCUM—Society for Cutting Up Men. *A late 1960s radical feminist group whose intention it was to eliminate, via sabotage, every facet of society that did not pertain to women.*

SWALCAKWS—Sealed With A Lick, 'Cause A Kiss Wouldn't Stick.

WIMPS—Weakly Interactive Massive Particles. *Remnants of the Big Bang.*

WOOPIES—Well-Off Older People.

XYZ—Examine Your Zipper.

YUPPIE—Young Urban Professional. *Attributed to columnist Alice Kahn, in 1983.*

Other Peculiar Acronyms

ACORN—Acronym-Oriented Nut. *Quoted in William Safire's column "On Language" in* The New York Times Magazine.

CAVE—Communities Against Virtually Everything.

DIED—Department of Industrial and Economic Development. *This Ohio department is now defunct.*

EGADS—Electronics Ground Automatic Destruct Sequencer. *U.S. Air Force system for destroying malfunctioning or approaching missiles.*

LIE—Long Island Expressway.

LORD—Let Oral Roberts Die. *The punchline of George Bush, Sr.'s joke about "a new fundamentalist group," told to an unappreciative audience of staunch conservatives in Lansing, Michigan, in Feb. 1987. It referred to Roberts's claim that if his church failed to receive enough donations, the Lord would take him home.*

PTL—Praise The Lord. *This televised ministry, headed by Jim Bakker, was nicknamed* Pass The Loot *by less-than-faithful viewers. After Bakker's 1989 conviction for bilking parishioners of over $150 million, the acronym was reinterpreted as* Prison Term Long, *although Bakker's original forty-five-year sentence was reduced to eighteen years, then to eight, and the televangelist was released from federal prison in 1994 after serving just five years.*

Oxymorons

Classic Oxymorons

Act natural.
Advanced BASIC Advanced Beginner's All-purpose Symbolic
    Instruction Code
alone together
Anarchy rules!
athletic scholarship
authentic reproduction/replica
awfully good/kind
a back door front (meteorological term)
black light
blues festival
building down (referring to nuclear disarmament)
business ethics
chicken-fried steak
civil war
Congressional leadership
deciding not to decide
dimwit
down escalator
drag race
dress pants
drink yourself sober
elevated subway
false truth
farewell reception
final draft
free with purchase
fresh frozen
full of holes
God-awful
Good grief!

graduate student
historical fiction
holy war
home office
Internal Revenue "Service"
It's bad luck to be superstitious.
killed alive
Labor Day holiday
laborious idleness
lay professional
light heavyweight
a little (bit) big/much
living end
maxi brief
a miss hit (table tennis term)
modern classical
Moral Majority
much/a lot less
negative growth
neoclassical/neo-/Gothic/traditionalist
never, ever
Now, then . . .
numb feeling
old news
open secret
original copy
paid volunteer
peacekeeping force/missiles
(*choose your number*) percent pure
permanent loan
plastic silverware/glass(es)
pretty ugly
pygmy mammoth (found in a 1994 archaeological dig)
random order
religious science
rolling stop
same difference
science fiction
scientific creationism
Scottish Danish (a pastry sold at 7-Eleven stores)
a sharp and blunt speech

shirtless and shoeless, with trousers to match

sight unseen

small fortune

sophomore (from the Greek *sophos*, meaning "wise," and *moros*, "foolish")

Still waters run deep.

super flyweight

terribly pleased

There are no absolutes.

thunderous silence

unsalted saltines

unscented incense

well-preserved ruins

whole piece

wintergreen

Quotable Oxymorons

- "Clichés are a dime a dozen: avoid them like the plague."
- "I'd give my right arm to be ambidextrous."
- "If I did say that, I was misquoted." —*Lord Hanson, "The World at One" (Radio 4, London)*
- "If you fall and break your legs, don't come running to me."
- "Give me the luxuries of life and I will gladly do without the necessities." —*Frank Lloyd Wright*
- "May I ask you a question?"
- "The more I think of you, the less I think of you."
- "perfectly wrong" —*NASA official referring to a defective mirror in the Hubble telescope in 1989*

Some Favorites

current history

drive-in exit

express line

extra low (*price*)

extraordinary

ivory black

marine airmen anagrammatic

"No comment."

objective opinion

pop culture
preventative medicine
sunshade
tomboyish girl (redundant)
turn(ed) straight
twelve o'clock in the afternoon
wireless cable

Word Ways Oxymoron Collection

by reason of insanity
a closet claustrophobic
dry lake
even odds
monopoly
objective journalism
Positively no!
spendthrift
split union
standard deviation; normal deviation
sure bet
turn up missing

Stage & Screen

Film Titles

- *Advance to the Rear* (1964), comedy
- *Death Benefit* (1996), starring Peter Horton
- *Dead Alive* (1993), horror film starring Timothy Balme and Diana Penalver
- *Faraway, So Close* (1993), fantasy starring Otto Sander
- *Hide in Plain Sight* (1980), crime drama starring James Caan
- *Little Big Man* (1970), novel by Thomas Berger (1964); film starring Dustin Hoffman
- *Little Giants* (1994), Duwayne Dunham film starring Rick Moranis
- *True Lies* (1994), starring Arnold Schwarzenegger and Jamie Lee Curtis
- *And Now Tomorrow* (1944), drama starring Loretta Young

Quotes from Stage & Screen

- On the army: "What other job lets you die for a living?"
  —*Hawkeye Pierce in* M*A*S*H*, *cited in Jack Mingo and John Javna's* Prime Time Proverbs *(1989)*
- "I'm an atheist. Thank God I've always been one." —*Spanish surrealist filmmaker Luis Buñuel*
- "In film, the best sound of all is silence." —*Faye Dunaway, on* Inside the Actor's Studio
- "When I'm good, I'm really good; but when I'm bad, I'm better." —*Mae West*
- "Everything I've ever told you has been a lie, including that." —*Peter Cook in the film* Bedazzled *(1967)*
- ". . . caught in the act of being themselves" —*Allen Funt, from the television show* Candid Camera
- "There's a broad with her future behind her." —*Constance Bennett on Marilyn Monroe*
- "I must be cruel, only to be kind." —*William Shakespeare's* Hamlet
- "undisputed boxing champion"—*George Carlin*
- "Last week I blew $5,000 on a reincarnation seminar. I figured, what the hell—you only live once." —*comedian Ronnie Shakes*
- "Don't miss it if you can." —*Traffic reporter Brian Ward, on* KKOB, *Albuquerque, New Mexico*
- "It costs a lot to look this cheap." —*Dolly Parton*
- "It takes a smart man to know he's stupid." —Lou Grant *television series, cited in Jack Mingo and John Javna's* Prime Time Proverbs *(1989)*

Politics & Diplomacy
The language of politics and diplomacy is always a rich source of oxymorons, circumlocutions, chop logic, and double-speak.

- "I intend to open this country up to democracy, and anyone who is against that, I will jail, I will crush!" —*1979 presidential speech by Brazil's General João Baptista Figueiredo*
- "Capital punishment is our society's recognition of the sanctity of human life." —*Utah Senator Orrin Hatch, 1988*
- "We must allow our soldiers to fight this war in peace."

- "violent peace" —*U.S. Navy reference to a limited armed conflict*
- "permanent pre-hostility" —*the Pentagon referring to peace*
- "peacekeeper" —*former U.S. President Ronald Reagan referring to the MX missile in a televised speech, Nov. 22, 1982*
- "Organize spontaneous cheering." —*public-relations manual for former U.S. President Jimmy Carter's 1976 campaign*
- "an incomplete success"—*former U.S. President Jimmy Carter when referring to the attempted rescue of American hostages in Iran*
- "I believe that this country's policies should be heavily biased in favor of nondiscrimination." —*former U.S. President Bill Clinton*
- Progressive Conservative —*formerly one of Canada's three major political parties*
- Revolutionary Institutional Party —*Mexico*

Literary Oxymorons

- "The coldest winter I've ever spent was a summer in San Francisco." —*Mark Twain*
- "It usually takes more than three weeks to prepare a good impromptu speech." —*Mark Twain*
- ". . . His honor rooted in dishonor stood, and faith unfaithful kept him falsely true." —*"Lancelot and Elaine" from Alfred, Lord Tennyson's* Idylls of the King *(1885)*
- "faultily faultless" —*Alfred, Lord Tennyson*
- "His only fault is that he has no fault." —*Pliny the Elder*
- "Mr. Gladstone has no redeeming defects." —*Benjamin Disraeli of William Gladstone*
- "He hasn't a single redeeming vice." —*Oscar Wilde*
- "To be natural is such a very difficult thing to keep up." —*Oscar Wilde*
- "Life is much too important a thing to ever talk seriously about it." —*Oscar Wilde*
- "Nature, to be commanded, must be obeyed." —*Francis Bacon*
- "scalding coolness" —*Ernest Hemingway*
- "melancholy merriment" —*George Gordon, Lord Byron*

- "proud humility" —*Edmund Spenser*
- "hateful good" —*Geoffrey Chaucer*
- "There is nothing in this world constant, but inconstancy." —*Jonathan Swift, in* A Critical Essay upon the Faculties of the Mind *(1707)*
- "What the crowd requires is mediocrity of the highest order." —*Auguste Préault, 19th-century French writer*

By Definition

These oxymoronic definitions are found in Ambrose Bierce's *The Devil's Dictionary* (1911).

habit "a shackle for the free"
Hades "the place where the dead live"
recollect "to recall with additions something not previously known"

In Quotes

ANDY WARHOL
- "I always run into strong women who are looking for weak men to dominate them."
- "I am a deeply superficial person."

WOODY ALLEN
- On life and death: "Eternal nothingness is OK if you're dressed for it."
- "I'm not afraid to die; I just don't want to be there when it happens."

GROUCHO MARX
- "'Military intelligence' is a contradiction in terms."
- In a letter to the Friars Club: "Please accept my resignation. I don't want to belong to any club that would have me as a member."

LEDERER'S OXYMORON COLLECTION
These treasures were found by Richard Lederer, author of *Crazy English* (1989) and other books on the discrepancies of our language.

baby grand
ballpoint
bridegroom
building wrecking
conspicuously absent
divorce court
loose tights
mandatory option
many fewer
nonworking mother
pianoforte (soft-loud)
press release
someone
speech writing
student teacher
superette (big-small)
wholesome
working vacation

"It takes about ten years to get used to your own age."

Oxymorons in Title & Song

MEMORABLE BOOK TITLES
- *Memories of the Future*: original title in German of Erich von Däniken's *Chariots of the Gods?* (1969)
- Oscar Levant's *The Memoirs of an Amnesiac* (1965)
- Elliot Richardson's *Reflections of a Radical Moderate* (1994)

SONG TITLES
- "Glad to Be Unhappy" —*Richard Rodgers and Lorenz Hart*
- "Happy with the Blues" —*Lyrics by Peggy Lee, music by Harold Arlen*
- "If You Won't Leave Me Alone, I'll Find Someone Who Will" —*Delbert McClinton and Glen Clark*
- "I Forgot to Remember to Forget" —*Stan A. Kesler and Charlie Feathers*
- "Atta-Boy, Girl!" —*Roger Miller*

- "The Sound of Silence" —*Paul Simon*
- "Earth Angel" —*a 1954–1955 hit by The Penguins*
- "Something Must Be Wrong Because Everything Is Going Right" —*Dr. Jazz*

SONG LYRICS
- "Now they know how many holes it takes to fill the Albert Hall." —*John Lennon and Paul McCartney's "A Day in the Life"*
- "I can't forget that I don't remember what." —*Leonard Cohen's "I Can't Forget"*
- "To live outside the law you must be honest." —*Bob Dylan's "Absolutely Sweet Marie"*
- "I was so much older then; I'm younger than that now." —*(redundant oxymoron) Bob Dylan's "My Back Pages"*
- *"His tail cut long"* —*"Where Has My Little Dog Gone?"*

LOVING YOU DROVE ME MAD

The Oxymoron Song
Here are the lyrics to my 1979 song "Loving You Drove Me Mad: The Oxymoron Song." It contains ten oxymorons.

> I lost my mind to win your heart,
> Knowing well we were off to a finishing start.
> I can't get into getting out
> 'Cause I'm quite certain about my doubt.
> I'm happy feeling sad,
> Loving you drove me mad.
> I turned you on, then you turned on me,
> When it came my turn, you turned away.
> I could never get used to getting used
> To do the things that you refused to.
> It's the blues, if I keep or lose you;
> Loving you drove me mad.
> Well, it takes a lot of the little I've got;
> I'm more confused the more I give it thought.
> I lost it all on one "sure bet,"
> Now I can't recall what I ought to forget.
> Let's just forget we've never met;

Loving you drove me mad.
Now, bad is good, and cold is hot,
It's a contradiction; then again, it's not.
I've given up all o' my sanity,
In search of some sweet memory,
But nostalgia isn't what it used to be;
Loving you drove me mad.
You're the best I've never had;
Loving you drove me mad.

Proverbs & Advice

Contradictory Proverbs

Look before you leap.
He who hesitates is lost.

It's better to be safe than sorry.
Nothing ventured, nothing gained.

If at first you don't succeed, try, try again.
Don't beat your head against a stone wall.

Silence is golden.
The squeaky wheel gets the grease.

Actions speak louder than words.
The pen is mightier than the sword.

Many hands make light work.
Too many cooks spoil the broth.

Two is company; three is a crowd.
The more the merrier.

Clothes make the man.
Don't judge a book by its cover.

You're never too old to learn.
You can't teach an old dog new tricks.

Absence makes the heart grow fonder.
Out of sight, out of mind.

Good things come in small packages.
The bigger, the better.

Like attracts like.
Opposites attract.

Great minds think alike.
Fools never differ.

When in Rome, do as the Romans.
Above all, to thine own self be true.

Do unto others as you would have others do unto you.
Nice guys finish last.

Revised Proverbs

A schoolteacher asked her seven-year-old students to fill in words she omitted from proverbs. Here are some of the surprises.

- "You can't have your cake and still be hungry."
- "Too many cooks cook."
- "Better late than last."
- "A miss is as good as a mister."

Of course, adults, though lacking children's innocence, modify proverbs, too.

- "Imitation is the sincerest form of television." —*Fred Allen*
- "Where there's a will, there's a relative." —*source uncertain*
- "One good turn gets all the blankets."
- "The shortest route to a man's heart is through his chest." —*Roseanne Arnold*
- "Cleanliness is next to impossible."—*a child's lament*
- "I cried because I had no shoes, until I met a man who had no class."

Reconstructing Glass Houses

Variations on: "People who live in glass houses shouldn't throw stones."

- "People who live in grass houses shouldn't stow thrones."
- "People who live in fur houses shouldn't throw stoles."
- "People who live in doghouses shouldn't throw bones."
  —*Al Roker*

Quips & Quotables
- "With fronds like these, who needs anemones?" —*Jazz musician Paul Desmond, admiring California palms and a friend's aquarium*
- "Graham Quaker" —*Richard Nixon, from a Quaker family, when he welcomed the support of evangelist Billy Graham in his 1968 presidential campaign*
- "Demons are a ghoul's best friend."
- "In America, cows don't get 'mad,' they get eaten." —*Garrison Keillor, Prairie Home Companion radio raconteur*

Old Standards
The last three of these revised old standards are my inventions.

- "A fool and his money are some party."
- "He's a wolf in cheap (or chic) clothing."
- "He's rusting on his laurels."
- "All's fear in love and war."
- "Abstinence makes the heart grow fonder."
- "He always ends a sentence with a proposition."
- "He's waiting for the right girl to come alone."
- "He sees all women as sequels."
- "He's dead and married."
- "A man cannot live in bed alone."
- "It takes two to tangle."

Original Aphorisms
Since proverbs and aphorisms can be coined by anyone, I thought I'd include a few of mine.

- "Life is too short to rush through."
- "I'm a contradiction, then again I'm not."
- "One problem with old age is that it's hard to reminisce about."
- "Tongue-in-cheek and foot-in-mouth go hand in hand."

Chapter 6

Words to Fear

You are probably familiar with the usual phobias, like agoraphobia or claustrophobia. Here are some others psychologists credit that may not be in your vocabulary, as well as a few names for phobias that haven't yet earned their place in the scientific lexicon.

Other Phobias

These phobia words are compiled from many sources, including Paul Hellweg's *The Insomniac's Dictionary* (1986). Alfred Hitchcock had *policophobia*. He never drove a car for fear of being ticketed by the police. Dweezil Zappa reportedly has *levophobia* while driving, and J. Edgar Hoover suffered from the same affliction. Hoover forbade his chauffeurs to make left turns.

The term *hydrophobia* is both "the fear of water" and the medical term for "rabies." There are two definitions of *lyssophobia*, "the fear of water" and "the fear of becoming hydrophobic," but, to my knowledge, there is no term for "the fear of lyssophobia." Here are some of the other lesser-known phobias.

alektorophobia chickens

apeirophobia infinity

aulophobia flutes

aurophobia gold

barophobia gravity

carnophobia meat

cherophobia gaiety

chronophobia time

dextrophobia things to the right

dikephobia justice

eleutherophobia freedom

euphophobia good news

gelophobia laughter

geniophobia chins

hedonophobia pleasure

heliophobia sunlight

hellenophobia cumbersome Greek or Latin words

homilophobia sermons

hygrophobia dampness or liquids, especially wine or water

ideophobia ideas

levophobia or **sinistrophobia** things to the left

linonophobia string

melophobia music

metrophobia poetry

odontophobia teeth

optophobia opening one's eyes

panophobia fears

papaphobia the pope

pentheraphobia mother-in-law

philophobia love

phronemophobia thinking

prosophobia progress

pteronophobia feathers

rhinophobia noses

selenophobia the moon

siderophobia stars

sophophobia learning

teratophobia monsters or giving birth to a monster

uranophobia heaven

venustaphobia beautiful women

vestiophobia clothing

Would-be Phobia Words

We have lots more in the world to fear than is found in the annals of psychologists and medical practitioners. Consider these.

aibohphobia palindromes

arachibutyrophobia peanut butter sticking to the roof of the mouth —*People's Almanac (1975)*

cacophonophobia bad music

corpulophobia, diametrophobia, expansophobia, radiaphobia widths

lunaediesophobia Mondays

omophagiaphobia, omositiaphobia eating raw flesh

paronomasiaphobia puns

phlebophobia blood tests

phobologophobia phobia words —*Paul Hellweg*

profundophobia depth

vacansopapurosophobia blank paper

Chapter 7

Mispronunciations & Misconceptions

Commonly Mispronounced Words

The following words all have common nonstandard or erroneous pronunciations. The peculiar preferences of Britspeak and Amerispeak—or indeed Aussie, New Zealand, Indian, Continental, Canadian, and French-Canadian English—account for some differences, but certainly not all. Hybrid speech and bilingualism can introduce odd, humorous, or puzzling inflections (and our pronunciations surely sound just as strange to the ears of those who speak with other accents).

asterisk AS-ter-ik, AS-trik

athlete ATH-eh-leet, ATH-uh-leet

bacterium (*singular*) bak-TEER-ee-uh (bacteria [*plural*])

barbiturate bar-BICH-oo-et

biathlon, decathlon by-ATH-eh-lahn, de-KATH-eh-lahn, etc.

criterion (*singular*) cry-TEER-ee-uh (criteria [*plural*])

deteriorate de-TEER-ee-ayt

drowned, drowning DROUN-ded, DROUN-ding

escalate ES-keuh-layt

escape ex-SCAYP

espresso ex-PRES-o

excerpt EK-sert, EK-zert, EK-serp, EK-zerp

foliage FO-lij, FOI-lij

heinous HAY-nee-us

intravenous intra-VEE-nee-us

jewelry JOO-ler-ee, JOO-luh-ree

larynx LAIR-nex, LAIR-eh-nex

memento moh-MEN-toh

mischievous mis-CHEE-vee-us

NASA NA-sah (Nassau)

nuclear NOO-kyuh-ler

phenomenon (*singular*) feh-NAHM-eh-nuh (phenomena [*plural*])

peripheral per-IF-ee-uhl

perspiration pres-per-AY-shun

pumpkin PUNG-ken

realtor REEL-eh-ter

Social Security SO-sha KYER-ih-tee, SOH-suhl she-KEYR-ih-tee

supposedly suh-POH-ziv-lee, suh-POH-zub-lee

surprise suh-PRYZ

valentine, Valentine's Day VAL-en-tym('s day)

Venezuela ven-zoo-AY-luh, ven-nuh-zoo-AY-luh

veterinarian vet-n-AIR-ee-en, vet-NAIR-ee-en

Wimbledon WIM-bl-ten

Misnomers

- *Guinea pigs* are not pigs and do not come from Guinea.
- *Blindworms* are legless lizards that can see.
- A *dressed chicken* is undressed.
- The *French phone* was invented by Robert Brown, an American.
- A *mosquito bite* is a puncture.
- *Caraway seed* is not a seed, but a dried fruit.
- A *silkworm* is a caterpillar.
- In *dry cleaning*, all articles are thoroughly saturated in a wet solution.
- The *jackrabbit* is a hare.
- The *Jerusalem artichoke* is a sunflower (*Helianthus tuberosus*).
- The *Pennsylvania Dutch* (really Deutsch) are German.
- *Catgut* strings are made from sheep intestines.
- *Bedstraw* is not straw, but an herb, formerly used to stuff mattresses.
- *Old Ironsides* sides were made of wood.
- *Hay fever* is not caused by hay, but by pollen.
- A *peanut* is neither a pea nor a nut, but a leguminous herb.
- *Arabic numerals*, also called *Arabic figures* (the numbers 1 to 9) were invented in India.
- *India ink* comes from China and did not originate in India.
- The country of *India* is officially known by its Hindu name, Bharat.

Coined Words, or Some that Should Be

affluential affluent and influential

Amereconomics the ultimate in capitalism

classive pertaining to class

crosstume a cross-dress costume

fileophile a lover of files

mediacracy government controlled by the media

parapsychosis the state in which a delusion is perceived by the subject as paranormal, or a disabling devotion to the supernatural; similar to *entheomania*: religious insanity

platinym a platitude synonymous with another, like "appearances can be deceiving" and "you can't judge a book by its cover"

realitize face reality; make real—carry out a plan or an idea; live out a fantasy

Accidental Injury

Moving Violations

These are alleged personal accounts from auto accident reports. All except the last three come from William G. Espy's collection in Willard R. Espy's *Another Almanac of Words at Play* (1980).

- "An invisible car came out of nowhere, struck my vehicle, and vanished."
- "The guy was all over the road. I had to swerve a number of times before I hit him."
- "Coming home, I drove into the wrong house and collided with a tree I don't have."
- "The pedestrian had no idea which direction to go, so I ran over him."
- "I had been driving my car for forty years, when I fell asleep at the wheel and had an accident."
- "A pedestrian hit me and went under my car."
- "The indirect cause of the accident was a little guy in a small car with a big mouth."
- "I saw the slow-moving, sad-faced old gentleman as he bounced off the hood of my car."
- "I pulled away from the side of the road, glanced at my mother-in-law, and headed over the embankment."

As I Was Saying . . .

- "If you aren't fired with enthusiasm, you'll be fired with enthusiasm." —*Vince Lombardi*

- "We are all in this alone." —*Peg Tuppeny in Paul Dickson's* The New Official Rules *(1989); also attributed to Lily Tomlin*
- "We must believe in free will; we have no choice." —*Isaac Bashevis Singer in his 1978 Nobel Prize for Literature acceptance speech*
- "It's not that I dislike many people; it's just that I don't like many people." —*Bryant Gumbel*
- "You've no idea what a poor opinion I have of myself, and how little I deserve it." —*Gilbert & Sullivan*
- "This report is filled with omissions." —*John Henrick,* Omni *magazine*
- "I'm not a snob. Ask anybody. Well, anybody that matters." —*Simon LeBon of the rock group* Duran Duran
- "That's what show business is—sincere insincerity." —*British comedian Benny Hill*
- "I think of myself as a 'resident out-of-towner.'" —*Calvin Trillin*

Kidspeak

- Hearing that adults around the breakfast table were having boysenberry syrup on their waffles, an 8-year-old asked: "Could I have some poison berries on my awful?"
- A five-year-old declared she likes her eggs "sunny side out."
- A boy explained that his faithful family dog is a "damnation" (dalmatian).
- A fourteen-year-old natural palindromist advised: "Egad, nab a bandage!"
- Influenced by 1960s television-commercial jingles, a nine-year-old girl thought the Immaculate Conception referred to pristine kitchen floors waxed by perfect housewives.

Chapter 8

Where's Your Grammar?

Five Tips to Better Grammar
Here are some takes on grammar rules you thought you knew.

1. Dangling from a sentence, one should always avoid leaving a participle. —*Marin Fischer*

2. Double negatives are no-nos. —*Bob Johnston in Paul Dickson's* The New Official Rules *(1989)*

3. Don't verbify nouns. —*David Means*, Mensa Bulletin, *Dec. 1995*

4. Don't use a preposition to end a sentence with.

5. And never start a sentence with a conjunction.

About rule 4, there really is no such grammar rule, but most writers and teachers avoid breaking it. About ending a sentence with a preposition, Sir Winston Churchill quipped: "This is the type of arrant pedantry up with which I will not put!" Berton Braley in "No Rule to Be Afraid of" mused: "The grammar has a rule absurd/ Which I would call an outworn myth:/ 'A preposition is a word/ You mustn't end a sentence with.'" Rule 5 also does not exist in any reliable grammar guide. In other words (my words), "It's okay to end a sentence with a preposition, if you *want* to."

Joan Rivers, on Grammar
Joan Rivers, in a commencement speech she gave in 1989 at her daughter Melissa's graduation from the University of Pennsylvania, said: "You're college graduates now, so use your education. Remember—it isn't who you know, it's whom."

Junior Preposition

Junior yells downstairs to ask his father to bring up a certain book and read it to him. Dad appears with the wrong book. Junior says: "Aw, whaddya bring that thing I don't wanna be read to out of up for?" —*Martin Gardner,* O&C *(1961)*

Write Advice

- "Never say 'never,' and always avoid 'always.'" —*John M. Hazlitt in* The New Official Rules
- "Be obscure clearly." —*E. B. White*
- "'Free verse' is like 'free love'; it is a contradiction in terms." —G. K. Chesterton

Ride & Walk

In Martin Gardner's *Oddities & Curiosities* (1961), Leigh Mercer provides this confusing sentence.

"How much better it is to ride in a car and think 'How much better it is to ride in a car than it is to walk' than it is to walk and to think 'How much better it is to ride in a car than it is to walk.'"

Misdemeanors

Many former grammatical felonies have been reduced to minor misdemeanors, or even decriminalized, in today's vernacular. A few ungrammatical phrases that have become common usage include "healthy diet" ("healthful diet"), "different than" ("different from"), "anxious to" ("anxious about" or "eager to"), "like I said" ("as I said"), and "like it is" ("as it is"). Other expressions that have crept into everyday speech are "hopefully" ("I am hopeful that . . ."), "more importantly" ("more important"), and the ever-present pseudo-suffix "-wise," as in "temperature-wise" and "time-wise."

Chapter 9

Spellcheck

Vowel Search

English Words Without Vowels
sh *or* shh
tsk tsk(s)
nth

The Longest English Word without an "E"
   Floccinaucinihilipilification, the longest English word without an "e," means "the action or habit of estimating a thing or an idea, etc., worthless" (*OED*).

Vowels in Alphabetical Order
   Words in current use containing the six vowels (*a, e, i, o, u,* and *y*) in alphabetical order include *abstemiously, affectiously, facetiously, half-seriously,* and *pareciously*. The words in this list contain the regular five vowels (*a, e, i, o,* and *u*) in order.

abstentious
acheilous (same as *achilous*)
acheirous
aerious (the shortest)
annelidous
arsenious (alternate spelling of *arsenous*)
arterious
atenisodus
bacterious
caesious
fracedinous
lateriporus
parepitoxus

More Ordered Vowels in Phrases
   In the word *adventitious*, the letter "i" is repeated. The longest terms containing the regular vowels in order seem to be

lawn tennis court and *watering trough*. Willard Espy in *Another Almanac* (1980) provides a sentence containing all the vowels in order: "Ann's bed is old but dry."

Chemical Symbols & Elements

Twelve chemical elements can be spelled using only elemental symbols. Puzzler Nightowl supplied this list in her puzzle newsletter *The Ag Mine*, quoted from *Chemical & Engineering News* (1993).

ArSeNiC
AsTaTiNe
BiSmUTh
CArBON
CoPPEr
IrON
KrYPtON
NeON
PHOsPHORuS
SiLiCoN
TiN
XeNon

Words in Numbers

- 100204180 translated into words reads: "I ought not to owe for I ate nothing."
- 280? Too weighty.

Numbers in Words

This fabricated ad first appeared in a 1968 Mensa publication, with numbers one through nine in order.

> "Want a wooden overcoat? Buy honest John Whitworth's health-re-energizing sulfo-uranyl-impregnated 'Comfi-Vest' with its unique quasi-xyloid fibers— obtainable only from the Paradise Vending Company, Harpurville Heights, Nineveh, New York."

Words in Numbers & Letters

Simple, but perfect examples of the "letter rebus" are IV (*ivy*), NV, SA, FND (effendi), SKP, NME, XLNC, and XPDNC.

Rebuses and other riddles were very popular in the 18th and 19th centuries. *The Youth's Companion*, Sept. 25, 1879, featured an "illustrated" or "pictorial" rebus of a man in a tent, lying tied to the top of the letters "X" and "L." Below the picture were these questions.

- Why is this man likely to succeed in life? (He is bound to XL.)
- Why do we know he has reached middle life? (He is over forty.)
- How does the picture indicate his occupation? (He is in tent on letters.)

Words & Letters in Words

Wordsmith Mark Saltveit refers to the *charades* in the right column as "redividers," a more descriptive term. "Barm aid," "is a belle," "on us," and "Reform a Tory" could be considered *oronyms*, words that sound like others.

- abalone—a "B"alone
- alkaline—Λl Kaline
- amiable together—Am I able to get her?
- "An 'A' to my—anatomy," said Adonis.
- attendances—at ten dances —*John Newton,* Merry's Puzzles *(1856)*
- barmaid—barm aid
- beauties—beau ties (bow ties)
- a caravan—a car, a van
- generations—gene rations
- handled—hand-led
- Isabelle—is a belle
- island—is land
- manslaughter—man's laughter
- mendicant—Mend, I can't.
- nowhere—now here
- onus—on us
- rampant—ram, pant
- reformatory—Reform a Tory.
- theirs—the IRS
- Wasted—was Ted!

More Charades

- A reversal charade: *Leno—One "l"*
- A *toreador* who had never learned *to read or* to write, when asked for his signature, gave this *significant* reply: "How can I *sign if I can't* write?" —*Dmitri Borgmann,* On Vacation *(1965)*
- English bibliographer William Oldys (1687–1761) wrote of himself: "In word and *will I am* a friend to you,/ And one friend *old is* worth a hundred new."

Sound Spelling

HOMONYMS, HOMOPHONES, & HOMOGRAPHS

The homonym *chase* means both "to pursue" and "to ornament metal." And then we have homophones, words with the same sound but different spellings. Consider *heir* and *air*, and, if you feel fanciful, *compassion* and *come, passion.*

These homonyms and homophones should not be confused with homographs, words spelled alike with different origins and meanings, whether they are pronounced alike or not. Examples are *homer*—"home run" or "unit of measure"; and *bat*—as in baseball, or bat, the animal.

HETERONYMS

The words *refuse* (re-FUSE) and *refuse* (REF-use) are spelled alike, but pronounced differently, have different meanings, and are derived from different roots.

Another example of a heteronym, found by Darryl Francis (*WW*, Aug. 1979), is *union-ized* and *un-ionized.*

Chapter 10

CONTRA-dictory TERMS

Pro & Con
An observant 19th-century wordsmith pointed out the prefixes of opposite meaning in the words *progress* and *Congress.*

Contranyms
A *contranym* or *contronym*, which is a recently coined term, means a word or an expression having two or more opposite meanings. This has also been called a Janus-faced word and the dictionary refers to it as an *antilogy.* Two homonymous contranyms are *raise—lift* and *raze* or *rase—tear down.* Here are classic examples of ordinary contranyms.

aloha Hawaiian for "love," used as "hello" and "farewell"

bimonthly every two months—twice a month (semimonthly)

bolt secure in place—dart away

bound restrained—to spring

buckle fasten—come undone

cheerio "hello"—"good-bye"

cleave adhere to—split or divide by force

commencement beginning—conclusion

dust remove fine particles from—sprinkle fine particles on

fast speedy—fixed firmly in place

give out produce—stop producing

handicap advantage—disadvantage

hold up support—hinder

impregnable invulnerable—able to be impregnated

left departed from—remaining

overlook fail to notice—examine

put out generate—extinguish

ravel entangle—disentangle

root implant firmly—remove completely

scan examine carefully—glance at or read hastily

screen view—conceal

seed remove seeds from—add seeds to

shank the latter part of a period of time—the early part

temper soften—strengthen

trim add to—cut away

vital lively; necessary to life—deadly; destructive to life

weather withstand—wear away

wind up start—end

Pseudo-Antonyms

- catwalk—dogtrot
- give in—take out
- give off/put off—take on
- give up/put up—take down

- hereafter—therefore
- hotheads—cold feet
- inning—outing
- input—outtake
- layout—stand-in
- left off—Right on!
- lowlands—high seas
- maternity dress—paternity suit
- nighthawk—mourning dove
- overlay—understand
- sit(-)in—stand out/standout
- undergo—overcome
- walk-on—run off/runoff
- walkout—run(-)in
- walk-up—run(-)down

Quasi-Antonyms

These *quasi-antonyms*, some from Tom Pulliam and Dmitri Borgmann in *WW*, have the same or similar meanings. Some dictionaries list *noninflammable*, a self-contained quasi-antonym.

- barred—debarred
- bone—debone
- burn up—burn down
- fat chance—slim chance
- fill in—fill out
- flammable—inflammable
- irregardless—regardless
- loosen—unloosen
- ravel—unravel
- restive—restless
- slow up—slow down
- unremorseless—remorseless

Pseudo-Synonyms

British wordsmith Peter Newby introduced *pseudo-synonyms* in WW, Feb. 1995, and Susan Thorpe, a fellow Brit, provided these examples.
- wind power—air force

- raindrop—waterfall
- Central Time—Middle Ages
- tall order—high command

Seeing Double

Mirror Words

Turn this page upside down before a mirror and read these words.

HIDE OXIDE CHOICE COD

Latin & Greek

It was rumored that President James Garfield was able to write in Greek with his left hand and Latin with his right, simultaneously.

Chapter 11

A Miscellany

Reverse Parallelisms

The *reverse parallelism* or *chiasmus* is a nifty literary device in which the second half of a sentence rephrases and turns around the first half. Psychologist Mardy Grothe's book *Never Let a Fool Kiss You or a Kiss Fool You* (1999) contains 2,500 examples. Here are a few from his collection.

- "Ask not what your country can do for you. Ask what you can do for your country." —*former U.S. President John F. Kennedy*
- "It's not the men in my life, it's the life in my men." —*Mae West*
- "Suit the action to the word, the word to the action." —*William Shakespeare*
- "I write better than those who write more quickly than I do, and quicker than those who write better than I do." —*A. J. Liebling*

Here is my best attempt at writing a reverse parallelism: "I can't get an edge in wordwise, let alone a word in edgewise." And here's a close relative of a reverse parallelism: "I fiddle with the violin, or you could say that I violate the fiddle." Some word-unit palindromic sentences in this book are similar to these. Consider: "You can cage a swallow, can't you, but you can't swallow a cage, can you?"

Word Ladders

By changing one letter at each stop, while keeping the other letters in the same order, these words can evolve into their opposites.

P U S H	P U L L
H U S H	P U L E
H U S K	R U L E
H U L K	R U S E
H U L L	R U S H
P U L L	P U S H

Lewis Carroll's Head to Tail

Lewis Carroll introduced this puzzle form, which he called *doublets* (our *word ladder*, previous page), in *Vanity Fair*, Mar. 29, 1879. These puzzles have also been called laddergrams, word chains, word links, step words, passes, and transformations. Here's Carroll's HEAD to TAIL.

```
H  E  A  D
H  E  A  L
T  E  A  L
T  E  L  L
T  A  L  L
T  A  I  L
```

In Short

Shortest English Poems

These shorts come from Martin Gardner's *Oddities & Curiosities* (1961). In Oct. 1925, the "Literary Review" column in the *New York Evening Post* featured this poem by Eli Siegel.

> ONE QUESTION
> I,
> Why?

This might be one of the shortest palindromic poems in English, written around 1960.

> REACTIONS TO A STATEMENT BY KHRUSHCHEV THAT THE SOVIET UNION HAS NO DESIRE TO MEDDLE IN THE INTERNAL AFFAIRS OF OTHER NATIONS
> O,
> So?

Shortest Bible Verse

"Jesus wept." —*John 11:35*

A Short Correspondence

Shortly after *Les Miserables* was published in 1862, Victor Hugo, eager to know how well his book was selling, sent his publishers, Hurst and Blackett, a note which read: "?" The publishers replied: "!"

Illogical English

The comedian Gallagher wonders:

- Why a building that is finished is not referred to as a "built"?
- Why one TV is called a "set"?
- Why one panty is considered a "pair"?
- Why a bra is seen as a single item?

Richard Lederer notes:

- "We recite at a play and play at a recital."
- "We drive on a parkway and park in a driveway."
- Tim Martin, *WF*, observes: *Proposition* is the long term for the short term, and *propose* is the short term for the long term.
- "Abbreviation is a 12-letter word."
- "*Monosyllabic* has five syllables."
- "A "near hit" is called a "near miss."
- "To be 'out for someone' is to 'have it in for someone.'"

Twisted Sentences

Pangrams

A *pangram* is a sentence containing all the letters of the alphabet. This one by Dmitri Borgmann in Martin Gardner's *Oddities & Curiosities* (1961) uses all letters of the alphabet just once:

"Cwm, fjord-bank glyphs vext quiz."

A cwm is Welsh for "a circular valley" (w is a vowel in Welsh). A glyph is a carved figure, vext is a poetic spelling for vexed, and a quiz is an 18th-century word for an eccentric. The sentence thus means: "Carved figures in a valley on the bank of the fjord irritated an eccentric person."

Maxey Brook's pangrams, *WW*, May 1987, use 43 letters:

"My girl wove six dozen plaid jackets before she quit."
"Her gift box of jigsaw puzzles quickly drove me nuts."

Howard W. Bergerson supplied this delightful 40-letter pangram:

"Xavier picked bright yellow jonquils for Mitzi."

Here are two more:

"Sympathizing would fix Quaker objectives." (36 letters)

"The five boxing wizards jump quickly." (31 letters)

Tongue-Twisters

- A little alliteration: "Are you copper-bottoming 'em, my man?" she asked. "No," he replied, "I'm aluminiuming 'em, mum."
- *Aluminium* is the British spelling of what Americans know as alumi-num. —O'London's, *Oct. 26, 1929*
- "Top step's pup's pet spot." —*Leigh Mercer's tongue-twister palindrome in Martin Gardner*, Scientific American, *Sept. 1964*
- "The rapid rabid rabbit ran rampant."

SEE-SAW

Mr. See and Mr. Soar were old friends. See owned a saw and Soar owned a seesaw. Now See's saw sawed Soar's seesaw before Soar saw See, which made Soar sore. Had Soar seen See's saw before See saw Soar's seesaw, then See's saw would not have sawed Soar's seesaw. But See saw Soar and Soar's seesaw before Soar saw See's saw, so See's saw sawed Soar's seesaw. It was a shame to let See soar so sore just because See's saw sawed Soar's seesaw.

ANOTHER SEA-SAW

Here is Eric Albert's offering of a false past tense:

seahorse; sawhorse

Idiomatic

Here are a few idioms, in the style of Bill Dana (aka José Jimenez), which never seemed to catch on.

- That pancake is flatter than a . . .
- Tea isn't my cup of . . .
- Those flies are dropping like . . .
- Those rabbits are breeding like . . .
- That doornail is deader than a . . .

Chapter 12

Anagrams in the Major Leagues

By Defininition

Anagrams, Transposals, & Mutations

An *anagram*, defined by the National Puzzlers' League, is a transposition of letters in a familiar word, name, or phrase into another, appropriate to the base. The NPL considers a *transposal* a reshuffling of letters in a name or dictionary-sanctioned word or phrase to form another, not necessarily related, word or phrase. Examples are: ERIC CLAPTON—"narcoleptic,"[1] SENATOR—"treason,"[2] RISE TO SPEAK—"strike a pose,"[3] and HERE AND NOW—"we're on hand."[4]

A *mutation*, by the league's definition, is a rearrangement of a word or set of words into another, not normally used, bearing little or no relation to the base. An example is INTEGRITY—"tiny tiger." Mutations were more popular in the 19th century than today.

Finding the Best

Basic Criteria

Several criteria can be used to judge the quality of an anagram. Experts usually agree that the ideal anagram:

1. refers clearly and specifically to the base,

2. uses standard English,

3. is transposed completely,

4. contains no extraneous or filler words, and

5. maintains parallel syntax, number, and tense with that of the familiar word, name, or phrase.

The anagram "has to pilfer," made from A SHOPLIFTER, is apt and well mixed, but does not stand on its own, parallel to the base in form, as does "a rich Tory caste," made from THE ARISTOCRACY. Since few anagrams are parallel, cohesive, apposite, and well transposed, this book includes many of the former type (A SHOPLIFTER "has to pilfer").

Some Rules of Exclusion

ALL IN THE THEME

Words that do not refer specifically to the theme detract from an anagram. The words *great* and *late great*, for instance, may be considered to detract from these anagrams about Edison and King. In THE GREAT THOMAS ALVA EDISON—"The good man, he lit vast areas." (Here the word *the* is repeated.) THE LATE, GREAT DR. MARTIN LUTHER KING—"Think tall! A dreamer greeting truth." Some puzzlers find the use of articles (*a, an, the*) acceptable in an anagram. Superfluous words often made from left-over letters are SIR(S), NOTE, and interjections such as O, OH, AH, HA, and LO.

WELL-MIXED LETTERS

An anagram of POETRY, "Try Poe," by Hoosier (*TE*, Mar. 1934) could also be seen as flawed because only syllables are transposed. Many anagram writers feel that the number of letters repeated in sequence should not exceed three; some consider this too restricting. Most veteran puzzlers agree that an anagram should not contain any words that appear in the base.

LENGTHY ANAGRAMS

George Haywood (1866–1887), a well-known puzzler of his day, pointed out that abnormally long anagram bases rarely yield good results because they tend to contain fewer words that refer directly to the subject(s). It is, however, easier to form a grammatical sentence from a long base because of the increased number of possible letter combinations.

JUST FOR EXERCISE

In this transposition exercise, I included the initials of my name to deal with the remaining letters, *O* and *M*. By adding the letters *R* and *E* to the base, I eliminated the need for initials, shown in the second example. Another criticism of the anagrams is that the bases are contrived.

> I'LL SETTLE FOR WRITING ANAGRAMS,
> arranging as letters will fit. —*O. M.*

> I'LL SETTLE FOR REWRITING ANAGRAMS,
> arranging as *more* letters will fit.

Some of my better attempts, without the aid of a computer program, all printed in *TE*, were OSCAR WILDE—"I lace words (A WRITER *of* rare wit)"; JACKIE MASON—"a manic jokes"; PLATAN—"a plant"; and A PSYCHIATRIST—"Sit, chat, pay, sir." ANGELIC—"nice gal" appeared in *WF*.

AVOIDING CONTRIVED BASES

The first two bases above are contrived, as is A CONE POUR-ING RED-HOT LAVA, which when shuffled can be made into "Oh, dear! A volcano erupting."

Here is a classic with a contrived base: A FORESTER REFERS TO "a fosterer for trees."[1]

In choosing anagrams for my top 50 list, I excluded those made from contrived bases, such as IN THE SOUTH SEA ISLANDS—"A thousand islets shine."[2]

HEADLINES & MISSING ARTICLES

Many anagrams read like newspaper headlines; they contain key words but omit the articles *a, an,* or *the.* The base and ana-gram STATE CRIMINALS—"a miscreant list" was an actual headline in a Jan. 1898 Pittsburgh newspaper. Anagrams for ISRAEL PUTNAM—"Salem Puritan,"[1] MOURNING—"grim noun,"[2] and DORMITORY—"dirty room"[3] relate well to the subjects.

However, I think that if the letter A could be used in these bases, without repeating the letter as a word, the anagrams would be enhanced. So, A DORMITORY would become "a dirty room." On the other hand, if it were possible to transpose DOR-MITORIES into "dirty rooms," the anagram would be parallel to the base and not require the article *a.*

CHESTER ARTHUR—"truth searcher"[4] would be improved grammatically, but not anagrammatically, by adding the initial of his middle name, forming CHESTER A. ARTHUR—"a truth searcher." Unfortunately, the word a in the base would also appear as a word in the anagram. In either case, "truth searcher" is too vague a description of Arthur's character and could apply to many other people. The same thing could be said about this amusing anagram, ROSS PEROT—"sore sport."[5]

One highly praised example is "Bear hit den," made from HIBERNATED.[6] The problem with that sentence is the missing article the, which makes it slightly ungrammatical. I prefer an anagram that reads as naturally as its base—in English as it is normally spoken or written.

ARTICLES AT LARGE

Many anagram bases contain what I consider forced use of the article the in place of a or an, as in THE NUDIST COLONY— "no untidy clothes"[1] and THE OVERCOAT—"cover to heat."[2] The article the seems grammatically unnecessary in these anagrams of plurals: THE CARDINALS—"in cathedrals,"[3] THE HURRICANES—"These churn air,"[4] and THE EYES—"They see." Although these break no grammatical rules, I prefer anagrams and bases in which the word the refers to a particular person, place, or thing, such as THE U.S. LIBRARY OF CONGRESS —"It's only for research bugs."

INTERJECTIONS

In culling my top 50 list of anagrams, I also omitted anagrams containing interjections, such as THE ZOOLOGICAL GARDENS— "Oh, gaze into droll cages!,"[1] A SEARCHLIGHT—"Ach! This glare!,"[2] and my favorites, GILROY, CA—"Garlic? Yo!"[3] and IT'S ALL GREEK TO ME—"Gee, talker, I'm lost."[4]

UNMIXED LETTERS & "I"

Not included in my list of choice anagrams are those with four or more unmixed letters, those inappropriately written in the first person, and those using the word I, when it refers to a non-person. Here are some of the best "I" anagrams I've found; all work as effective declarative sentences.

THE "I'S" HAVE IT

1. DISARMAMENT I'm at arm's end.

2. FRITO-LAY I fry a lot.

3. MAINE I am N.E.

4. DECIMAL POINT I'm a pencil dot.

5. MILITARISM a. I limit arms. b. I limit Mars. (Both are antonymous anagrams.)

6. THE LIQUOR HABIT Quit! I rob health.

7. A POLICEMAN'S WHISTLE I am seen with all cops.

8. UNITED STATES BUREAU OF FISHERIES I raise bass to feed us in the future.

A MATTER OF CHOICE

My main criteria for choosing the anagrams in the list of Fifty Choice Anagrams were historical content, humor, longevity of subject matter, and names, phrases, or terms that are commonly known or could be found in current reference books.

Of the thousands of anagrams I have scanned, many contain antiquated words and expressions or forgotten names and events. William Walsh, in his *Handy-Book of Literary Curiosities* (1892), stated: "After centuries of endeavor, so few really good anagrams have been rolled down to us. One may assert that all the really superb anagrams now extant might be contained in a pillbox." Although many "choice anagrams" have been written since Walsh's time, there are fewer than one might expect, considering that over a century has passed.

Puzzlers and the public, however, have shown renewed interest in anagrams and palindromes. Many early forms of these elegant trifles have been included in this book. Most were found in periodicals, including *The Enigma* ("in the game") and *The Eastern Enigma*. Many come from Ross Eckler's *The New Anagrammasia* (1991).

Other word puzzlers may not share my criteria, or biases, for determining an anagram's quality. Choosing anagram examples, therefore, is necessarily subjective, no matter how strict one's criteria. Although nearly all anagrams listed here were composed as puzzles, many were judged from a grammatical point of view.

Fifty Choice Anagrams

Here are fifty well-composed anagrams.

1. AIRFIELDS aid fliers.

2. AN AISLE is a lane.

3. ANIMOSITY is no amity.

4. THE ARISTOCRACY, a rich Tory caste.

5. ATHLETICS, lithe acts.

6. THE COMPULSORY EDUCATION LAW You must learn; police do watch.

7. CONSIDERATE Care is noted.

8. THE COUNTRYSIDE, no city dust here.

9. DESPERATION A rope ends it.

10. DESTINATION It is to an end.

11. EARNESTNESS a stern sense.

12. EDGE TOOLS good steel.

13. EXECUTIONS exits on cue.

14. THE EYES They see.

15. FATHER TIME, a term thief.

16. GOURMET more gut.

17. THE HOLY GOSPEL helps theology *or* theology's help.

18. INNOMINATE no name in it.

19. THE LANDING OF THE PILGRIMS English, in flight, made port.

20. THE LEANING TOWER OF PISA What a foreign stone pile!

21. THE LOST PARADISE, Earth's ideal spot.

22. MINISTERS remit sins.

23. NO TRESPASSING Stop an ingress.

24. OLD MASTERS, art's models.

25. ORCHESTRATE. Score the art.

26. PASTORSHIP, parish post.

27. PENURIOUSNESS no use in purses or no purses in use.

28. PITTANCE, a cent tip.

29. POSTPONED Stopped? No.

30. PRO-LIFE Flip Roe.

31. RECEIVED PAYMENT; every cent paid me.

32. RED TAG SALE Great deals!

33. ROME WAS NOT BUILT IN A DAY Any labour I do wants time.

34. PROSPERITY is property.

35. SAINTLINESS, least in sins.

36. A SENTENCE OF DEATH faces one at the end.

37. A SHOPLIFTER has to pilfer.

38. A SIGNAL OF DISTRESS It's SOS read in flags.

39. SKIN CARE irks acne.

40. SOUTHERN CALIFORNIA, hot sun or life in a car.

41. A STRIP TEASER spares attire.

42. SUGGESTION It eggs us on.

43. SURGICAL INSTRUMENTS, smart curing utensils.

44. THEOLOGICAL SEMINARIES Sole aim: teach religions.

45. THREE-POINT-TWO, the "wet" portion.

46. TRADESMEN need marts.

47. UPHOLSTERERS restore plush.

48. THE U.S. LIBRARY OF CONGRESS It's only for research bugs.

49. WASHINGTON CROSSING THE DELAWARE He saw his ragged Continentals row.

50. WESTERN UNION, no wire unsent.

Honorable-Mention Anagrams

These fifty honorable-mention anagrams seem flawed or do not appeal to my particular tastes. Many bases in these anagrams contain the grammatically unnecessary word *the*. Two of the anagrams are outdated, and a few contain alternate or non-standard spellings (*venders, rime, learnt,* and *rassle*), but they're still noteworthy.

1. ACETAMINOPHEN, the "no-pain" acme?

2. ADVERTISEMENTS Items at venders.

3. THE ARCHEOLOGIST He's got a hot relic.

4. THE ARTESIAN WELLS Water's in all these.

5. ASPERSION, no praises.

6. THE ASSASSINATION OF PRESIDENT ABRAHAM LINCOLN A pistol in an actor's rebel hands; a fine man is shot.

7. THE ASTROLOGER He got star lore.

8. BARGAIN HUNTERS Run, grab in haste!

9. BASTARDS, sad brats.

10. THE CARICATURE, caustic art here.

11. THE CARICATURISTS Their art's caustic.

12. THE CHINESE RESTAURANT Taste Hunan's rice there.

13. THE COLLEGE UNDERGRADUATES Our "green" shall get educated.

14. THE COMPLETE WORKS OF WILLIAM SHAKESPEARE Pick Marlowe; ask if *he* wrote all these poems.

15. FAMILIES, life's aim.

16. THE DAWNING Night waned.

17. DESEGREGATION Negroes get aid.

18. DOMESTICATED ANIMAL, docile, as man tamed it.

19. DROMOMANIA Mad, I roam on.

20. THE EDUCATION TELEVISION PROGRAMS Video teaching primes us to learn a lot.

21. EQUESTRIAN, equine arts.

22. GARBAGE MAN, bag manager.

23. "GATHER YE ROSEBUDS WHILE YE MAY." (Robert Herrick) Here's why beauty goes dim early.

24. THE GERMAN SOLDIERS Hitler's men are dogs!

25. HUSTLERS Let's rush!

26. INNUMERABLE, a number line.

27. INTELLIGENTSIA, an elite listing.

28. THE INTERNATIONAL MORSE CODE Those radio men once learnt it.

29. THE LANDSCAPE GARDENER He planted ranged acres.

30. LIMERICKS, slick rime.

31. THE LORD'S DAY Add holy rest.

32. THE MARIMBA Hammer a bit.

33. MICHELANGELO BUONARROTI'S CREATION OF ADAM A Roman ceiling, too, can house formidable art.

34. THE OLD-AGE PENSION helps one in dotage.

35. AN OLD SHOE had no sole.

36. ONE-ARMED BANDITS, Reno's damned bait.

37. THE POULTRY DEALERS They do rear pullets.

38. THE PROFESSIONAL WRESTLER No sport left where I rassle.

39. THE SATURDAY NIGHT SPECIAL, a gun they list as dirt cheap.

40. THE SEPTUAGENARIAN, near that supine age.

41. SNOOZE ALARMS Alas, no more Zs.

42. "A STITCH IN TIME SAVES NINE." This is meant as incentive.

43. A SURGICAL OPERATION Pain or gore, alas, I cut.

44. THE TAM-O'-SHANTER That's no mere hat!

45. TELEVISION NEWS It's now seen live.

46. "TO CAST PEARLS BEFORE SWINE" One's labor is perfect waste.

47. TOTAL ABSTAINERS sit not at ale bars.

48. THE UNITED STATES OF AMERICA So much in a tea fee started it.

49. VALENTINE POEMS, pen mates in love.

50. THE VOLCANIC ERUPTIONS stir each plutonic oven.

Less Perfect Anagrams

Although each of these anagrams contains four or more unshuffled letters, they are too interesting to exclude.

1. APPROPRIATENESS is apt, sane, proper.

2. DISARMAMENT Amend it, Mars.

3. THE INFERNAL REGIONS No final resting here!

4. IVANHOE BY SIR WALTER SCOTT, a novel by a Scottish writer.

5. THE KNOW-IT-ALLS We think so tall.

6. NOVA SCOTIA AND PRINCE EDWARD ISLAND, two Canadian provinces, lands I dread!

7. OPERATION DESERT STORM made one terrorist stop.

8. THE PROFESSIONAL GAMBLER He'll bear profits on games.

Anagram Varieties

One-Word Anagrams

Here are apt single-word transpositions, many of which could be called synanagrams, a term coined by Murray Pearce in *WW*, Aug. 1971. LAUDATION—"adulation" contains five unmixed letters. "Prenatal" has been called an anagram of PATERNAL and PARENTAL, but by NPL standards, it would be considered a transposal. "Reductions" would be a more appropriate anagram of DISCOUNTS, if that were possible. Other one-word anagrams in this list which could be criticized are INAMORATA—"amatorian," IT'S—"'tis," and SABBATH—"shabbat." TAP—"pat," which are phonetic reversals, seem to be among the few non-palindromic English words that are synonymous forward and backward. This one-word anagram list could include the popular reversals AH!—"Ha!" and OH!—"Ho!"

IN A WORD

1. ADOBE abode.

2. ANGERED enraged.

3. APT pat.

4. DEDUCTIONS discounted.

5. DETOUR routed.

6. DISCOUNTER reductions.

7. EVIL vile.

8. FIANCÉS fancies.

9. HEIGHTS highest.

10. INAMORATA amatorian.

11. INGESTA eatings.

12. IT'S 'tis.

13. LAUDATION adulation.

14. LISTERIZE sterilize.

15. MARS arms.

16. PATERNAL parental.

17. RAISE arise.

18. RESCUES secures.

19. SABBATH Shabbat.

20. SHRUB brush.

21. STUM must.

22. TAP pat.

23. TONE note.

24. TOURING routing.

25. YEA! Aye!

Anagram Shorts & Transpositions

TRANSPOSED COUPLETS, OR PAIRAGRAMS

Here are some *transposed couplets*, or *pairagrams*. "Marine airmen" could be considered antonymous and oxymoronic. In the British magazine *Games & Puzzles*, Sept. 1975, a diversion called double anagrams was based on the same idea. Clues suggested answers that would be two-word transposals of each other. Well-mixed examples include the clue "hidden promise" with the answer "latent talent" (also used here); the clue "object in outer space" with the answer "remote meteor"; and the clue "seagoing craft" with the answer "ocean canoe." *Ocean kayak* is a valid term, but *ocean canoe* is not, to my knowledge.

1. Actors co-star.

2. American Cinerama.

3. best bets.

4. continued unnoticed.

5. coordinate decoration.

6. Elvis lives.

7. float aloft.

8. horse/shoer (one word).

9. latent talent.

10. marine airmen.

11. married admirer.

12. Oriental relation.

13. outer route.

14. Scat, cats!

15. stayed steady.

16. steno notes.

17. streaming emigrants.

18. team mate (also written as one word).

19. tramline terminal.

20. veto vote.

Triplet, or Trianagram

If pairagrams are admissible, then perhaps we can include a *trianagram*, which uses three terms that are anagrams of one another and reads as a sentence. You may prefer to add an article to the beginning of Eric Albert's sentence: "Discounter introduces reductions."

Antigrams—Antonymous Anagrams

Transpositions opposite in meaning to an original word or phrase are sometimes called *antigrams*, a term coined by Sans Souci in *Ardmore Puzzler*, Sept. 22, 1900. There are far fewer of these than conventional anagrams. That's probably because most appear to have been discovered accidentally by the composers. One of my favorite topical examples is MONDALE— "Dole man," referring to the 1976 U.S. vice-presidential candidates Walter Mondale and Robert Dole (Larry, *TE*, Oct. 1976).

The first antigrams labeled antigrams were published in *AP*, Nov. 17, 1900. Because the coined term *antigram* could also be understood as a shortened form of the term *antigrammatic(al)*, the opposite of *grammatical*, perhaps another term would be helpful. Maybe we could call them antonymograms, antonymous anagrams, or simply opposite anagrams.

Here are some antigrams, which can be considered antonymous anagrams.

1. ANTAGONIST not against.

2. DEMONIACAL a docile man.

3. DORMITORIES tidier rooms.

4. DYNAMITED a tidy mend.

5. EVANGELISTS evil's agents.

6. HIBERNIANS banish Erin.

7. HONOREES no heroes.

8. INROADS no raids.

9. THE MORNING AFTER in great form then.

10. THE OSCAR NOMINATION It's not a cinema honor.

11. THE PARSONAGE so pagan there.

12. PERSECUTED due respect.

13. PROTECTIONISM nice to imports.

14. REFORESTATION no fair to trees.

15. SAINTLINESS entails sins.

16. A SUN WORSHIPER I shun Ra's power.

17. SWELTERING HEAT the winter gales.

18. UNITE(D) untie(d).

19. THE VOLSTEAD LAW had all "wet" votes.

20. WITHIN EARSHOT "I won't hear this."

Ambigram

The term *ambigram*, an anagram ambiguously apposite or opposite in meaning from its base, was coined by Sibyl (Judith Bagai), former *TE* editor.

> THE NUCLEAR REGULATORY COMMISSION
> Your rules clone atomic nightmares![1]

> G. DUBYA Bad guy[2]

Transposals

The longest transposition of one scientific word into another found so far, is HYDROXYDESOXYCORTICOSTERONE—"hydroxydeoxycorticosterones" (27 letters), which is a variant spelling of the same word.

Of a nonscientific word, we have REPRESENTATIONALISM—"misrepresentational" (19 letters).

The first containing 18 letters was by Mephisto in *TE*, Sept. 1980: NATURAL NECESSITIES—"inarticulatenesses."

This was matched by Xemu in *TE*, June 1997: SECONDARY QUALITIES—"quasiconsiderately."

The longest well-mixed transposal is thought to be CINE-MATOGRAPHER—"megachiropteran" (15 letters), found by Hercules, *TE*, Dec. 1927.

One of Albert's favorites was EARL OF COVENTRY (a card game)—"olfactory nerve."

According to puzzlist and author Maxey Brooke, the earliest published transposal known was MITE—"time," by Matilda in the July 16, 1796 issue of the New York magazine, *The Weekly Museum.*

COTARNINE, an organic base, is obtained by the oxidation of NARCOTINE, a crystalline alkaloid extracted from opium.

ORLEANS is a city in France, and SALERNO, in Italy.

The letters of the name of the independent republic in Italy, SAN MARINO, also form ROMANIANS.

Film star MYRNA LOY and educator MARY LYON shared the same letters in their names, as did record producer RAY STARK and singer KAY STARR.

IRISH PECANS, shuffled, becomes SPANISH RICE; unfortunately, the former term only exists in this transposal.

In Sept. 1978, *The Wall Street Journal* reported that a motor oil manufacturer called XONEX was sued by EXXON for using the same letters in its name. Incidentally EXON (not EXXON) was coined for the company by Dmitri Borgmann.

TRIPLETS

Eric Albert found what is considered the longest well-mixed triple transposal: UNISON INTERVALS—NONUNIVERSAL-IST—INVOLUNTARINESS (15 letters).

He also discovered one of the best triple transposals: CECROPIA MOTHS—PHOTOCERAMICS—COMPOSITE ARCH (13 letters).

Chapter 13

Sense & Nonsense Anagrams

Anagrams, after all, invite a sense of play, but they are also governed by the laws of letters, each letter being carefully appointed to its place. Here are some anagrams on familiar themes and some to amuse you.

Anagram Musings

Consider: Through the magic of letter-shuffling, a BENGALI can be transformed into a BELGIAN, WILD BOARS into RABID OWLS, the game of POLO into POOL, and a MELON into a LEMON. The word SANITARY can be transposed into the opposite anagram NASTY AIR. But by adding the prefix IN- to the base, an apposite anagram can be made: INSANITARY then would become IN NASTY AIR.[1]

Chronological Liar

A thirty-two-year old who tells you he is in his early twenties might just be dyslexic, but a person spelling out FORTY-FIVE as their age would make an anagrammatist suspicious. Rik Edwards's *Longman Anagram Dictionary* (1985) shows that these letters conceal the words and age OVER FIFTY.

"Related"

The solution to these clues in verse from Malcolm Tent, *TE*, Apr. 1995, is an anagram containing four unmixed letters: "We're a family for peace, yet there's always a war on./ We could say the word is an oxymoron."

> DAMN KIN!
> MANKIND

Cheaters' Anagrams

1. *IDEALISTIC* italicised (British spelling).

2. "QUESTION?" in quotes.

3. MISSPELLINGS simpl, singels.

4. ROAST TURKEY? Try our steak.

Anagrammatic Cross-References

1. SEPARATE (see "apart").

2. INFIDEL (find "lie").

3. OPERAS (re: soap).

4. TELEVISION SET (see "it's not live").

5. DEFENSE (see "fend").

Hurry to the Rear

Eric Albert called my attention to this type of anagram, a "cyclic transposition," which shifts the first letter, c, to the end.

1. CABARET a bar, etc.

2. CABINET a bin, etc.

Diabolical Transformations

An article, "On Anagrams," published in *Belgravia* magazine, Sept. 1896, declared that Great Britain's promising offspring, Tasmania, was much to be commiserated. The name was changed to Tasmania from Van Diemen's Land, since it sounded somewhat diabolical in origin. It is clear, however, that His Infernal Majesty will not lightly yield his dominion, for in TAS-MANIA we find the startling announcement: "I am Satan."

Saint, Santa, Satan

1. SANTA Satan.

2. A SAINT I, Satan.

Anagram Puzzles

The number of letters for each word of the solution to the anagram puzzle is shown in parentheses after the puzzle, except when all letters of the clue are used to form a single-word answer. Asterisks indicate capitalized words. No clues are given to the single-word bases. The solutions are on p. 97.

1. I'm any martial. (1 8 3)

2. minus lace

3. I tap, I slug. (1 8)

4. flour and oats (7 5)

5. Name this famous path. (3 7 2 *6)

6. All right, a hint: a demented TV wit. (TV show title: 4 5 4 5 9)

7. trees, for a hint (3 4 6)

8. hint: hotel (3 *6)

9. hint: Leo (3 4)

10. She isn't Leo. (3 7)

11. cat; no Leo. (2 6)

12. often a fun dream (4 3 7)

13. a very hidden author (*5 *5 *7)

14. Swen or Inga (*)

15. AAU term

16. Spend it.

17. Idle? Sure!

18. time taxers

19. on any screen (*4 *7)

20. Topic: cone, lava, ruin (1 8 8)

A Few by the Numbers

At least three *apposite numerical transpositions* have been found, using contrived bases. The first, by Emmo W. (*TE*, Apr. 1948), is in English, and the last two, by Lee Sallows (*WW*, Feb. 1992), are in Spanish.

ELEVEN + TWO = twelve + one
CATORCE + UNO (14 + 1) = once + cuatro (11 + 4)
DOCE + TRES (12 + 3) = trece + dos (13 + 2)

A Year in Rhyme

Here are three poems containing all the letters in the names of the twelve months; Rev. Arthur Cyril Pearson may have written all three. The first includes the poem title in the anagram. It is from his *20th Century Standard Puzzle Book* (1907) and probably appeared in the *London Evening Standard* column years earlier. The second poem was in Rev. Pearson's article "Anagrams, Ancient and Modern," *Chambers's Journal*, Feb. 24, 1900. We've titled it "Merry." These two poems inspired the optimistic third verse we've titled "Inspiration," found in Rev. Pearson's *20th Century Book of Puzzles* (1915).

A POEM
Just a jury by number
Each scrap of year—
A number recording
Every jumble, tumble, tear.

MERRY
Merry, durable, just grace
My every future month embrace;
No jars remain, joy bubble up apace.

INSPIRATION
Burst, joybud, happy let me be,
Come turn, brave year!
A grumbler's murmur I can face,
Enjoy a jeer.

Unite-Untie in Verse

A *telestich* poem is one in which the final letters of the lines form a word. In this poem, a *double acrostic*, the letters at both the beginning and the end of the lines form a word. The two words here—*unite* and *untie*—make an opposite anagram. This poem, published in *N&Q*, Oct. 12, 1861, was written by Louisa H. Sheridan (d. 1841), who has been referred to as "the rival of Tom Hood in talent and wit." The French term *goût* means "taste, style, or preference."

Unite and untie are the same, so say yoU;
Not in wedlock, I ween, has this unity beeN;
In the drama of marriage, each wandering goûT
To a new face would fly, all except you and I,
Each seeking to alter the 'spell' in their scenE.

The Long & Short of It

The shortest anagrams in English, OH!—"Ho!" and AH!—"Ha!," are also reversals and palindromes when read as couplets. The latter anagram, written by Palea, was quoted in *GD*, June 4, 1898.

The base of the next anagram, about the Declaration of Independence, is somewhat contrived, but it is one of the best of the long examples. The author is Ann S. Thetics; it was printed in *TE*, Jan. 1924.

SIGNING OUR DECLARATION OF INDEPENDENCE OF THE UNITED STATES OF AMERICA Thirteen Colonies post defiance dead against future foreign dominance.

In the book *Of Anagrams* (1862), Henry Wheatley stated that the longest specimen he had found was in Spanish, on the Marques de Astorga and all his titles, from Francisco de la Torre y Sebil's *Luces de la aurora días sol* ("Lights of Daybreak"), containing eight lines of about 140 letters.

On Hearst

John Winkler's biography of William Randolph Hearst tells how the *New York World* once copied from Hearst's *New York Journal* an obituary on one "Reflipe W. Thanuz." THANUZ was the phonetic spelling of "the news" and REFLIPE W. was "we pilfer" spelled backwards. A reviewer of Winkler's book recalled that the *New York World* retaliated by inserting the name "Lister A. Raah" into a story. After the *New York Journal* had printed the story, it was pointed out that the name was an anagram of HEARST A LIAR. Martin Gardner describes these events in *Oddities & Curiosities* (1961).

Solutions to "Anagram Puzzles"

(from pages 93–94)

1. a military man.
2. masculine.
3. a pugilist.
4. natural foods.
5. the Isthmus of Panama.
6. "Late Night with David Letterman."
7. the rain forest.
8. the Hilton.
9. the lion.
10. the lioness.
11. an ocelot.
12. fame and fortune.
13. Henry David Thoreau.
14. Norwegians.
15. amateur.
16. stipend.
17. leisured.
18. taximeters.
19. Sean Connery.
20. a volcanic eruption.

Chapter 14

Palindromes

Running Back Words

A *palindrome* is a word, phrase, or number that reads the same backward as forward; the word comes from the Greek *palindromos*, which means "running back again." The first palindromic sentences in English were printed in 1614.

Sotades & Muses

The palindrome has also been called an *inversino, cancrine, reciprocal,* or *Sotadic* or *Sotadean* phrase or verse, after the third-century B.C. Greek poet Sotades. The poet was said to have degraded his muse by devoting his verse to harsh and vulgar satire. Legend has it that he wrote a poem lampooning his ruler, King Ptolemy II Philadelphus, who, in retribution, had him sealed in a box and dumped into the sea.

Sotadea carmina became the term for derisive verses, which probably were complimentary when read in the opposite direction. These verses were in the form of *word-unit palindromes;* in these each word is taken as a unit, rather than each letter. Although Sotades has long been associated with the palindrome, no palindromes were found in the few surviving fragments of his poems.

Accolades to the Palindrome

A coherent palindromic sentence is more difficult to compose than an anagram (an apposite transposition). Robert Thomsen in *Games, Anyone?* (1965) went so far as to say: "If you are able to create one simple sentence that is a perfect palindrome, yours is a life well spent." In 1929, a competitor in the column "Prose & Verse Competitions" of the London weekly *Everyman* wrote: "A palindrome may seem a simple problem on the surface, but as a matter of fact it is difficult enough to tax to the utmost the sharpest of wits."

Some of the best-known palindromes are these: "Able was I

ere I saw Elba" in Charles Bombaugh's *Gleanings* (1867). "Madam, I'm Adam" from Henry Wheatley's *Of Anagrams* (1862); and "a man, a plan, a canal, Panama!" by Leigh Mercer, *N&Q*, Nov. 13, 1948, which could have been considered as a tribute to George Washington Goethals, Panama Canal builder.

Palindromes would also seem to generate palindromes, just as literary quotes generate other quotes through decades and even through centuries. A palindrome echoing Mercer's original, "a mar on a panorama," written by T. H., appeared in *Ardmore Puzzler*, July 1899. Thirty years later, a palindromist named Lubin came up with "a dog, a panic in a pagoda" in *Everyman*, Nov. 28, 1929. Around 1970, J. A. Lindon penned "a dog, a pant, a panic in a patna pagoda." Closer to Mercer's theme was Edward Wolpow's "A man appals—I slap Panama." On former U.S. President George Bush's invasion of that country in 1989 came the palindrome "a man, a pain, a mania, Panama." John Agee in *Go Hang a Salami—I'm a Lasagna Hog* (1991) rephrased the familiar formula, "a car, a man, a maraca."

A Palindrome Collection

Letter-Unit Palindromes

Many palindromes collected here were found in rare magazines, books, and newspapers. Several are from G. R. Clarke's *Palindromes* (1887), which contains thirty-three examples, twenty-two illustrated by the author. Some come from *Ardmore Puzzler*, a privately issued magazine published from 1899 to 1909; the newspaper column "Complications" from the *Inter-Ocean*, both the Chicago daily and Sunday editions, in the late 1890s and 1906; and "Enigmatic Oddities" in the *Pittsburgh Post* in 1900. *The Enigma*, a popular source for palindromes, was called *The Eastern Enigma* before 1920.

Many palindromes are from Dmitri Borgmann's *Language on Vacation* (1965) and *Beyond Language* (1967), and Howard Bergerson's *Palindromes & Anagrams* (1973). J. A. Lindon and Leigh Mercer were major contributors to Borgmann's and Bergerson's books. Mercer (1893?–1978) joined the NPL in 1952 under the palindromic pseudonym of Roger G. M'Gregor.

Other sources include Martin Gardner's *Oddities & Curiosities* (1961), Charles Bombaugh's *Gleanings from the Harvest Fields of Literature, Science & Art* (1867–1890 editions), John Pool's *Lid off a Daffodil* (1982), Stephen Chism's *From A to Zotamorf* (1992), Jon Agee's *Go Hang a Salami* (1991), Jon Agee's *So Many Dynamos (& Other Palindromes)* (1994), Joaquin and Maura Kuhn's *Rats Live on No Evil Star* (1981), Rev. Arthur Pearson's *Pictured Puzzles & Wordplay* (1908), and Jeff Grant's *The Palindromicon* (1992).

Michael Donner's "Six I's" is a particularly interesting example because it also works as "IIIIII," from his 1996 book *I Love Me, vol. I*, which is itself a palindrome, with the subtitle *S. Wordrow's Palindrome Encyclopedia*. Many of the palindromes by John Connett have not been previously published.

Because palindromes, like folklore, have many versions and variations, often anonymously composed, it may be nearly impossible to find the original authors. Many palindromes collected here come from the earliest-known sources. Unattributed palindromes are anonymous. Sometimes palindromes seem to write themselves, often with unfortunate results for the subjects. Others, when collected, create witty dialogue or the stuff of radio drama.

FIRST WORDS

1. **a.** Adam: "Name me man."
   b. The Creator: "Name Me, man."

2. **a.** "Madam, (it is [in Eden] I sit.) I'm Adam."
   b. Eve: "Eve."

3. "Now Eve, we're here, we've won."

4. Mad, a detail of Eden: one defoliated Adam.

5. Cain, a (mono)maniac.

6. **a.** Eve damned Eden, mad Eve!
   b. Mad (at) Adam!
   c. Name Pa "ape man."

7. **a.** Eve is a sieve!
   b. Even Eve?

ALL AT SEA

8. **a.** "Pull up, Eva, we're here. Wave, pull up!"
   b. "Pull up if I pull up."

9. **a.** Delia sailed, Eva waved, Elias ailed.
   b. Delia sailed as a sad Elias ailed.
   c. "Sail, Elias."

10. **a.** "No word," I say, as I'd row on.
    b. No word, no bond, row on.

11. "Nora, a raft! Is it far, Aaron?"

12. "Raft far."

13. "You bet! I sure can omit Tim on a cerusite buoy!"

RIGHT, BUT NO CIGAR
14. **a.** "Cigar? Toss it in a can, it is so tragic." / But sad Eva saved a stub.
    b. Cigar Tom made ting in a can ignited ammo. Tragic.
    c. Cigar tosser: I fret, fall ill, after fires so tragic.
    d. Cigar to son? O so tragic!

DRINKS ALL AROUND
15. "Here so long? No loser, eh?" [Still on that barstool?]

16. Put (it) up.

17. Tip it.

18. **a.** "Yo! Bottoms up! U.S. motto, boy!"
    b. Campus motto: "Bottoms up, Mac!"
    c. Ban campus motto: "Bottoms up, MacNab."

19. "Ron, I'm a minor."

20. "No sot, nor Ottawa (legal age) law at Toronto, son."

21. "Lager, sir, is regal!"

22. "Regal was I ere I saw lager."

23. **a.** Drawn I ginward.
    b. "O gin, on (, on) I go!"

24. **a.** Stewed, a jade wets.
    b. Last call! It's late, yet Al still acts Al!

25. **a.** Not sober (re: Boston).
    b. "Pure" Boston did not sober up.

26. Nog eroded Oregon.

SPORTING CHANCES
27. "Yes, a call, a bat, a ball, a Casey!"

28. "SNAFU? Oy, Boston! O do not sob, you fans!"

29. **a.** "Boston, O do not sob."
    b. Boston did *not* sob.
    c. "I did not sob, Boston, did I?"

30. So many dynamos!

31. **a.** "Now (I see, referees), I won."
    b. "Now I nod; egged on, I won."
    c. "No, *we* won."

LITTLE WARS
32. **a.** "Now, sir, a war is won!"
    b. A war at Tarawa.
    c. "Now, sir, a war is never even, sir, a war is won!"

33. "Nam? Raw war man."

34. "Hanoi, dare we use radio? Nah."

35. Live wartime did emit raw evil.

36. Erin (is) in ire.

37. Able foe of Elba?

38. "Able was I ere I saw Elba."

39. Elba, Rome, memorable.

40. Poor troop! A side divided is a poor troop.

41. Ed is on *no* side.

42. Dumb mobs bomb mud.

43. a. "Draw, O Caesar! Erase a coward!"
    b. "Draw, O Howard!"
    c. (drawn inward)
    d. "Draw, O coward!"

44. "Sir, I soon saw I was no Osiris."

FOOD, GLORIOUS FOOD
45. a. Stressed? ([or]) Stress, Ed?) Not on desserts.
    b. No lemon(s), no melon.
    c. "I saw desserts, I'd no lemons, alas, no melon; distressed was I."
    d. "Stressed was I, sad, alas, to order a redroot salad as I saw desserts."
    e. "Salad, alas."
    f. "Boredom à la mode, Rob?"
    g. Desserts I desire not, so, lost one, rise distressed.
    h. "Norah's dessert, Sid, distressed Sharon."
    i. "Desserts, sis?" Sensuousness is stressed. [a mutual passion for sweets]
    j. "Stressed, Flo? Wolf desserts!"
    k. Stressed? No tips? Spit on desserts!

46. a. Stir grits
    b. Ma handed Edna ham.
    c. O slaw, also!
    d. "Doc, note, I dissent. A fast never prevents a fatness. I diet on cod."
    e. "Dish Sid a radish. Sid?" "Mash Sid a radish, Sam."
    f. (No!) Not a ton (on)! / Note! Not one ton.
    g. "Spoon it in. Oops!"

h. "Won ton? (No, Don.) Not now."
i. "May we nab a new yam?"
j. "Ana, nab a banana."
k. "Ana nabs Bob's banana."
l. "Yo, banana boy!"

WINE, WOMEN, & SONG

47. "Deny me not: atone, my Ned."

48. a. "Ned, I am now a won maiden."
b. "Now, Ned, I am a maiden won."
c. "Now, Ned, I am a maiden nun. Ned, I am a maiden won."

49. "Ma is a nun, as I am."

50. a. "Norma is as selfless as I am, Ron."
b. *Shortened versions:* "Norma, I am Ron." "Ma is as selfless as I am."

51. Harass (selfless) Sarah?

52. "Madame, not one man is selfless; I name not one, madam."

53. a. Rail (at a) liar!
b. "Rail on, O liar!"
c. Liars (, alas,) rail.

54. a. "Can I attain a C?"
b. Egad! A base tone denotes a bad age!
c. "Treble, Delbert?"
d. "Mother at song. No star, eh, Tom?"
e. "If I had a hi-fi!"
f. La, not atonal!
g. "Eton, for one tenor of 'note.'"
h. "Ron, Eton mistress asserts I'm no tenor."
i. Gnostic, a tacit song.

55. "Sex, Rex? A trap, Artaxerxes."

56. Party (booby) trap!

57.   Sex? Even a Dane vexes!

58.   Sol led Rob to hot bordellos.

59. a. I saw Ed under Deb's bed; red, nude was I.
   b. Ed, I hiss, "A lass I kiss, a lass I hide."

60.   "Revolt, love!" raved Eva. "Revolt, lover!"

61. a. Won't lovers revolt now?
   b. Revolt? No. Will I kill? I won't, lover.
   c. Revolt a fat-lover?

62. a. Ed, is Deb bedside?
   b. "Deb, smash Sam's bed!"
   c. "Deb, ignore me!" Ron gibed.
   d. Deb sat in Anita's bed; /Ned sat in Anita's den,/but Anita
   sat in a tub.

63.   "Did Eve peep?" "Eve did."

64.   Anna: "Did Bob peep?" Bob: "Did Anna?"

65. a. "Did I disrobe Jeb or Sid?"—"I did?"
   b. Deb or Sid was, I saw, disrobed.

66.   "O, desire! Rise, do!"

67.   "Rise, lame male! Sir?"

68. a. "Sex at my gym taxes!"
   b. ("Naomi), sex at noon taxes!" (I moan).

69.   "I moan, ('Live on, O evil,') Naomi!"

70.   Revere her ever!

71. a. "Ned, go gag Ogden."
   b. "Lace me, Portia! Wait! Rope me, Cal!"
   c. Egad! No(body do) bondage!
   d. "Wo, Nemo! Toss a lasso to me, *now!*"

e. "Tie it."
f. "Noose?" "Soon."
g. "Lash Sal!"
h. "Nail Ian!"
i. "Nail, Lillian!"
j. Knock! Conk!
k. Reliant nailer!
l. "Slap my gym pals."
m. "Eh? Cane my men, odd one?
n. No's in unison.
o. "Want serene rest? "Naw."

72. a. Sores? Alas, Eros.
b. Eros saw I was sore.
c. "Eros! Sidney! My end is sore."
d. "Sore dermis! I'm red, Eros."
e. Red? No wonder!
f. So renowned, I, a maiden, won Eros.

ECOLOGY
73.   To Lake Erie rim, all a mire; I reek a lot!

74.   We passed Odessa. Pew!

75.   A mar on a panorama.

76. a. Niagara, O roar again!
b. Niagara, eh? I hear again!

ALL DRAWN OUT
77. a. "Eva, can I stab bats in a cave?"
b. "Eva, can I evade Dave in a cave?"
c. "Eva, can I put a Manet (torn, rotten, a mat) up in a cave?"

78. a. Trades opposed art.
b. No, it is (opposed. Art sees trade's) opposition.
c. Trade ye no (mere) moneyed art!
d. Trades abased art.
e. Tram "art?" [graffiti]
f. He traded "art,"eh?
g. Pop art's trap = op. [art]

79. "Degas, are we not drawn onward, we freer few, drawn onward to new eras aged?"

80. An era came: Macarena (and went).

81. "Did Dean aid Diana?" "Ed did."

82. "Did I draw Della too tall, Edward?" "I did?"

WHO'S THERE?
83. Ed is busy. Subside!

84. "Al, let's go hog Stella."

85. a. Al lets Della call Ed "Stella."
　　b. A "Lola?"

86. a. "I did, did I?"
　　b. "He did, eh?"

WHODUNIT?
87. a. Stella won (dered:) no wallets(?).
　　b. Stella won (dered: "Roy ordered) no wallets?"

88. Rev.: "Ned, Nina made Ed a 'man' in Denver."

89. a. "Did Hannah say as Hannah did?"
　　b. "No, son."

90. "Did Ione take Kate?" "No, I did."

91. "Did I, ameliorating Nita, roil Ema?" "I did?"

92. "Did I fish? Tim's rod or Smith's, if I did."

93. "Did I do, O God! Did I as I said I'd do? Good, I did!"

94. a. Marge lets Norah see Sharon's telegram.
　　b. Marge let a moody baby doom a telegram.
　　c. "No telegram," Marge let on.

95.   Norah's moods (, alas,) doom Sharon.

96.   Della called.

SNOOPS
97. a. "Oh, who was it I saw, oh who?"
    b. "Oh, who was in a VW van I saw? Oh, who?"

98.   Nosy son!

99.   Was it a (bar or a) bat I saw?

100. a. "A rod. Not a bar, a baton, Dora."
    b. "Not a bastion? No, it's a baton."
    c. "No, it's a bastion."
    d. Dora sees a rod.
    e. No, it's a bar of gold—a bad log for a bastion.

UNDONE
101.   Not *seven* on a mere man, *one* vest on!

102.   Stiff fits?

103.   No dresser, Don!

104. a. "Got a tog?"
    b. "Anita got a toga, Tina."

105.   "Massive Levi's, Sam!"

106.   Tug at a gut.

INVASION & EVASION
107.   "Sue," Tom (smiles, "Selim) smote us."

108.   "Dammit, I'm mad!"

109.   "Max, I stay *away* at six a.m.!"

110.   "Evade (*me*,) Dave?" / "Evade (no one,) Dave."

111. "He won't, ah, *wander*, Edna. What now, eh?"

112. "Marc, scram!" *or* Marc: "Scram!"

113. "No, sir, away! A papaya war is on!"

YOUR MONEY OR YOUR LIFE
114. A *lawyer named* Otto made Ned a motto; (read with #115)

115. *Si nummi immunis.* ("Give me my fee and I warrant you free.")

116. See? Few owe fees.

117. Pay on time, emit no yap.

118. Borrow or rob.

119. Too long no loot.

120. Stole lots.

121. Sue us!

122. Must sell at tallest sum.

123. **a.** "Sums are deified, Erasmus."
   b. Sums are not set as a test on Erasmus.

124. Sad? I'm Midas!

FLEEING MADNESS
125. **a.** "Mad? Am I, madam?"
   b. "No, old loon!"

126. **a.** "Nurse, I spy Gypsies! Run!"
   b. Nurses run.

127. **a.** I roam as a Maori.
   b. I roamed under it as a tired, nude Maori.

128. a. Too far (, Edna, we wander) afoot.
   b. Too flat! A fatal foot.
   c. Too fat a foot!

129.   Selim's tired. No wonder, it's miles.

130.   "I did not limp, Milton, did I?"

131.   I run in Uri.

132.   "I'm runnin'!"—Nurmi

133.   Yale ran (in) a relay.

AUTOSHOP
134. a. Race pony? Nope, car.
   b. One car race, no?

135. a. A Toyota (race car)? A Toyota?
   b. A Toyota's a Toyota.

136.   Race fast, safe car!

137. a. 'Tis in a DeSoto sedan I sit.
   b. O, ram a Camaro!

138.   Gateman sees name, garage man sees name tag.

BIG MAN ON CAMPUS
139. a. Was raw tap ale not a gag at one lap at Warsaw?
   b. Was a raw tap ale not a reviver at one lap at Warsaw?

140.   "Hey, no mere ceremony, eh?"

141.   In a regal age ran I.

DIAMONDS & JADES, JACKS & MAIDS
142.   Diamond light, Odo, doth gild no maid.

143.   Eve saw diamond, erred; no maid was Eve.

144.   Deb, Boris eyed a jade. Yes, I too, Otis, eyed a jade. Yes, I robbed.

NET RESULTS
145. a.   Ten animals I slam in a net.
    b.   Net torn, even rotten.
    c.   Net safe—rotten net to refasten.

PEELINGS
146.   Emil asleep, Hannah peels a lime.

147. a.   "Emil, a sleepy baby peels a lime?"
    b.   "No, Mel, a sleepy baby peels a lemon."

148.   Sleepy Liza lazily peels.

149.   R. E. Lee, potato peeler.

"YOU" DO IT
150.   "We'll let Dad tell Lew." *or* "Si, we'll let Dad tell Lewis."

151.   "Lew, Otto has a hot towel."

152.   Dump mud.

153.   Draw no dray a yard onward.

154.   Draw putrid dirt upward.

155.   Till it, O Toro. Rototill it!

156. a.   Bog dirt up a sidetrack carted is a putrid gob.
    b.   Live dirt up a sidetrack carted is a putrid evil.

POLITICS AS USUAL
157.   Won't S.A.L.T. last now?

158.   Wonder if Sununu's fired now.

159. a.   Retract (it), Carter!
    b.   Won't Carter retract now?

c. Do-gooder, retract! Carter, redo! O God!
d. Retracting, I sign it "Carter."
e. To last, Carter retracts a lot.

160. a. O Democrat(s) star, come, do!
    b. Star comedy (by) Democrats!

161. a. Rise to vote, sir.
    b. Name now one man.
    c. Now Lon Nol won.
    d. Now rely, Tyler won.

162. a. Taft: fat.
    b. Want fat Taft? Naw.

163. Bob's a snake; Kansas Bob. [former senator Dole]

164. Sparta's one rule: lure no satraps!

165. Dubya won? No way, bud. [in Florida, 2000]

WATERGATE
166. Pure vocal lips spill a cover-up.

167. Hoopla cover-ups must suborn, in robust sums, pure vocal "pooh."

IRAN-CONTRA
168. North gift? Casey era? C.I.A.'s or Bush's law? Walsh sub rosa? I care, yes! Act! Fight Ron!

PANAMA, 1989
169. A man, a pain, a mania, Panama.

170. a. Noriega casts a cage: Iron.
    b. Noriega can idle, held in a cage—iron.
    c. Age, irony, Noriega.

171. A foray far from home/ This is how George will now / rewrite a palindrome: "A man appals. I slap Panama."

PERSIAN GULF WAR

172. a. Drat Saddam, a mad dastard!
   b. Mad dastard, a sad rat—Saddam.
   c. A red rat, Saddam! A mad dastard era!
   d. Mad dash, eh, Saddam?

BOSNIA

173. a. Bosnia: Pain. Sob.
   b. Bosnia gasps again! (sob).

GOING PLACES

174. An ole crab was I ere I saw Barcelona.

175. a. O, Grafton, not Fargo!
   b. Not Eton!
   c. "Not Cohocton!"
   d. "Not New York!" Roy went on.
   e. Low at New York, Roy went AWOL.

176. Ned, go to hot Ogden!

177. O go to Togo!

178. Oh . . . to go to Togo, tho?

179. O go t'Boston, not (sob) Togo!

180. Haiti? Ah!

181. a. "No, sir, (prefer) prison."
   b. "Golf? No sir, prefer prison flog."

182. a. Viva! Let no evil revel, ever. Live on, Tel Aviv!
   b. Viva, le Tel Aviv!

183. One (resort rose): Reno!

MARTHA, AMY & MA

184. "Here, help Martha. Ah! Trample her, eh?"

185. "Amy, must I jujitsu my ma?"

186.   "Ample help, Ma?"

ABOUT ROSES
187.   "Lapses? Order red roses, pal."

188.   "Red roses run no risk, sir, on nurse's order."

189.   Red Rose; madame's order.

190. a. "No misses ordered roses, Simon."
    b. "(E)no misses ordered roses, Simon(e)."

TAN OR HIDE
191. a. Sun at noon, tan us.
    b. "Wanna tan?" "Naw."

OUTERSPACE
192.   Tons of UFOs? Not.

193.   Hell, a spacecraft farce caps all, eh?

194.   SPACESUIT! (I use caps.)

TAKING STEPS
195.   Pour Dan is in a droop.

196.   Now I draw an award I won!

197. a. Step on no pets.
    b. Step not on pets.

SOMETHING FOOLISH
198.   'Tis Ivan, on a visit.

199.   I'm a fool—aloof am I.

200.   Drab as a (fool, as aloof as a) bard.

201.   Is it I? It is I.

202.   Diana saw Dr. Awkward was an aid.

203.   Avid (as a) diva.

OOPS!
204. a.   Pupils slip up.
     b.   "Pupils!" I say, as I slip up.
     c.   An error, Rena.

205.   Pa's a sap.

206.   A new order began; a more Roman age bred Rowena.

207. a.   Egad, Loretta has Adams as mad as a hatter! Old age?
     b.   Old? Lo!

GOOD & EVIL
208.   Deny a God, O gay Ned?

209.   Allah, lave Valhalla!

210.   St. Simon sees no mists.

211. a.   No evils live on.
     b.   No evil's deeds live on.
     c.   No evil sagas live on.

212.   No devil's deeds lived on.

213.   Lived on decaf, faced no devil.

214. a.   Dog-deifiers reified God.
     b.   Dog as a devil deified, lived as a god.

215.   "God as all!" I saw it, felt it, left; I was ill as a dog.

216.   Ah, Satan, no smug smirk rims gums on Natasha.
                 (*Natasha* is a diminutive of *Natalie*, "Christmas child.")

217.   "Satan, oscillate my metallic sonatas!"

218.   Revered now, I live on. O did I do no evil, I wonder? Ever?

219. Did Bob live evil? Bob did.

220. Live on, O do! to do no evil.

221. a. Live on (tenet:) no evil.
     b. Live not on evil.
     c. Live not on evil, madame; live not on evil.

222. "Reviled did I live," (said I, as) evil I did deliver.

223. Do Good's deeds live on? No, Evil's deeds do, O God!

PARTING WORDS
224. To the Devil: "Live, O Devil, revel ever; live, do evil!"

225. To the Deity: "Do, O God, no evil deed; live on, do good!"

Creating Pals

Earliest Palindrome

John Taylor, author of the earliest-known palindromic sentence in English, wrote: "This line is the same backwards as it is forward, and I will give any man five shillings apiece for as many as they can make in English: 'Lewd did I live & evil I did dwel.'"

Taylor's palindrome was found in Nathaniel Butler's *The Nipping or Snipping of Abuses* (1614). The ampersand (&) used to be a letter of the English alphabet, and from the 1300s to the 1600s, *dwel* was an acceptable spelling of our modern *dwell*. An updated version of his palindrome would read: "Evil I did dwell; lewd did I live."

Longest Palindromic Words

According to the *Guiness Book of World Records* (1993), the longest palindromic words (excluding *solutomaattimittaamotulos*, a quadruple compound Finnish word, "the result from a measurement laboratory for tomatoes) is the coined term *saippauk(ivi)kauppias* (19 letters), which means "a dealer in lye" (caustic soda). The word, said to be Finnish, was derived from the German word *seife* ("soap") and *kauppias*, from *kaufer* ("buyer or dealer") or *kaufen* ("to buy"). The longest palindromic word published in the United States is *kinnikinnik* (one of eight spellings), of Algonquinian origin, meaning "that which is mixed" (a mixture of bark, dried leaves, and sometimes tobacco, formerly smoked by Indians and pioneers of the Ohio Valley). Other long palindromic words in English are *redivider*, *repaper*, and *reviver*.

David Morice holds the record for the longest English word used in a palindrome: *antiparasympathomimetically* (27 letters).

Foreign-Language Palindromes

Dutch *"Mooie zeden in Ede,' zeei oom."* ("'Nice customs in Ede,' said Uncle.")

Finnish *"Nisumaa oli isasi ilo aamusin."* ("The field of wheat was your father's joy in the morning.") *"Isa, ala myy myymalaasi."* ("Father, don't sell your shop.") *"Nalli laukee taas; saat eekua lillan!"* ("The detonator is exploding again; your butt will be toasted!")

French *"Etna, lave devalante."* ("Etna, spreading lava.") "A l'autel elle alla. Elle le tua là." ("To the altar she went. She killed him there.")

German *"Bei leid lieh stets heil die lieb."* ("In sorrow, love always lent security," *or* "In trouble, comfort is lent by love.") This appears in Charles Bombaugh's *Gleanings* (1875).

Greek *"Niyon anomhmata, mh nonan oyin."* ("Wash your sins, not only your face." *or* "Purify the mind as well as the body.") Compare this to the second verse in Psalm 51: "Wash me thoroughly from mine iniquity, and cleanse me from my sin." It is believed that the Greek inscription dates back to the sixth century. It was found on a baptismal font in Hagia Sophia in Istanbul, Turkey.

Icelandic *"Allar munum ralla."* ("We shall all have a wild time.")

Italian *"Ove regnai piangere vo."* ("I go to weep where I once ruled.")

Latin *"Acide me malo, sed non desola me, medica."* ("Disgustingly I prefer myself, but do not leave me, healing woman.") *"Si nummi immunis."* ("Give me my fee and I warrant you free.") The translation is by William Camden in *Remains* (1605).

Portuguese *"Atai a gaiola, saloia gaiata!"* ("Tie the cage, naughty rustic girl!")

Spanish *"Sobornos son robos."* ("Bribes are robberies.") *"Sacara maracas."* ("He will take out the maracas.") *"Osos, somos soso."* ("Bears, we lack flavor!") *"Anita lava la tina."* ("Anita [little Anne] washes the bathtub.") *"Yo de todo te doy."* ("I give you a bit of everything.") The first three—about bribes, maracas, and bears—are by Mark Saltveit.

Swedish *"Ni talar bra Latin."* ("You speak good Latin.")

Welsh *"Lladd dafad ddall."* ("Kill a blind sheep.") This palindrome in *N&Q*, July 7, 1853, was written a year earlier.

Bilingual Palindrome

In March 1866 *Our Young Folks* magazine featured this remarkable English and Latin palindrome, contributed by James C. P., which has the same meaning in both directions: "Anger? 'Tis safe never. Bar it! Use love! *Evolves ut ira breve nefas sit; regna!*" ("Rise up, in order that your anger may be but a brief madness; control it!") The palindrome is not in classic Latin.

Latin Defense

"On Palindromes," *New Monthly Magazine*, 1821: "For the most beautiful example, we must turn to the annals of our own country (England), and to a woman. In the reign of Queen Elizabeth, when the education of women rendered them frequently superior to the other sex, a lady (of nobility) being banished from the Court on suspicion of her being too familiar with a great lord in favor, gave this device: The moon covered by a cloud, and the following palindrome for a motto: '*ablata at alba*'—'obscured, but pure.'" The magazine continues, "This kind of composition was never in any example of which we know so heightened by appropriateness and delicacy of sentiment."

William Camden in *Remains* (1605) gave the palindrome as "*ablata & alba*." Other translations of the palindrome were "banished but blameless" and "out of sight, but still white."

Chapter 15

Playful & Bewitching Pals

More Palindromic Amusements

Cats & Dogs

About cats and dogs, in anagrams we have SCAT—CATS![1]; GREYHOUND—"Hey, dog, run!"[2]; and STAGHOUND—"A dog hunts."[3]

Palindromists offer us "Revolt a cat lover" by Dale Reed in *Science Digest*, Feb. 1983; "Stack cats" in Jon Agee's *Go Hang* (1997); "Stacy's super-aware pussy cats!" poem by James A. Lindon in Howard Bergerson's *Palindromes & Anagrams* (1973); and by anonymous writers, "Senile felines?" and "We mew." About dogs, we have "Go, dog!"; "Dog, as a devil deified, lived as a god," from Rev. Arthur Pearson's *Pictured Puzzles & Wordplay* (1908); and "God save Eva's dog!" by Neil "Fred" Picciotto.

Musical Palindromes

Many musical palindromes have been composed, but I am aware of only one song in which the melody and lyric are palindromic. It is the Spanish: *"Somos o no somos."* ("Are we, or are we not?") According to *Palindromist*, spring 1997, the song was performed at a New York party thrown by Jon Agee to celebrate his book *So Many Dynamos!* (1994).

Mickey Mackenzie, a Michigan musician, composed an instrumental jazz piece, "Gnostic Illicit Song," that must be played with the chord progression "A-B-C-B-A."

Addition

Dave Morice provides this palindromic response to the anagram "ELEVEN + TWO = twelve + one."

> One + nine = nine? No.

A Hoot

Molemi wrote the palindrome "too hot to hoot," printed in the column "In Mystic Mood," *Farmer's Wife*, May 1911. Fill in the missing letters indicated by asterisks for the palindrome.

> 'Twas a night succeeding days
> Of Midsummer's fiercest blaze,
> Silent as a graveyard ghost
> Sat an owl upon a post.
> "Come," said I, "O strigine fowl!
> Why so silent? Speak, O owl!"
> The owl gave just one glance at me:
> "*oo *o* *o *oo*, to whoo!" said he.

Another Owl

Jon Agee in *Go Hang* (1991) gave us the palindrome "Mr. Owl ate my metal worm."

Versifying the Palindrome

These three verses, written by Tut (James I. Rambo) in the 1970s and published in *TE*, conclude with palindromes (italicized). The custard palindrome (without the verse) first appeared in G. R. Clarke's *Palindromes* (1887).

> Quiche Lorraine?
> Oh, not again!
> *Drat such custard!*
>
> Make it more simple!
> No puzzler's atrocity
> Stays afloat long on a flood
> Of verbosity.
> *Edit, damn it! Solemn word ties lessen;*
> *I drown wordiness, else it drown me;*
> *Lost in mad tide.*
> From moral heights unscaled by ardent beaux,
> Our miss still contemplates her blameless bed;
> Though supplicants abhor these pesky woes,
> The florist suffers most—when all is said!
> *Sir! I rose. No men, as late pained rage lapses.*
> *Order red roses, pale gardenia petals, anemones, or iris!*

Palindromic Names

Adaven, Nevada a community in Nye County, Nevada

Anuta Catuna Olympics contender and winner of the New York Marathon

Aoxomoxoa title of a 1969 album by the Grateful Dead

Apollo, PA Pennsylvania town cited by Enavlicm, *TEE*, June 1912

Dr. Awkward Dr. Michael Awkward, University of Pennsylvania English professor, found by Jon Agee

Emily's Sassy Lime teenage southern California punk trio

Kavon Novak a suggested, but discarded pseudonym for film star Kim Novak (b. Marilyn Novak)

Leon Noel French ambassador to Poland before World War II

Live Evil a 1983 record album by the rock band Black Sabbath

Lon Nol president of Cambodia from 1970 to 1975 (d. 1985)

Ogopogo alleged sea creature of Lake Okanogan, British Columbia, referred to as the (North) American Loch Ness monster. The first documented sighting of the creature was in 1852. The creature's name does not come, as many had supposed, from any language of Pacific Coast tribes found in the province. It may have been derived from a 1920s British music hall song.

Olé ELO! record album title by the Electric Light Orchestra

Omaha, MO town in Missouri

Revilo P. Oliver (III) professor emeritus, University of Illinois at Urbana

Robert Trebor Two actors were born with this name. One, better known as Bob Trebor, was also an announcer and talk show host on San Francisco's KGO radio.

"SOS" (by Abba) a 1976 hit song and the Swedish group who recorded it

Sydney Yendys the pen name of English poet Sydney Dobell (1824–1874)

UFO Tofu record album title by Béla Fleck & the Flecktones

U Nu prime minister of Burma from the late 1950s to the early 1960s

Wolf Flow a 1992 horror novel by K. W. Jeter

Businesses

Yreka Bakery, which has a palindromic name, baked bread in Yreka, California, for over a century. According to *American N&Q*, Jan.5, 1889, it was owned by a certain S. Gilligs (palindromic name). This establishment's name, mentioned in *Our Young Folks*, Mar. 1866, dates back more than 130 years. The editor of "Our Letter Box" column in *Our Young Folks* called such palindromes *inversions*.

West Miner Street, in Yreka, had two businesses with palindromic names. Next to the bakery was the **Yrella Gallery**. At last report, the gallery was still in operation.

Elite Tile is the name of chain stores that sell tile.

Famous Names in "Games"

In April 1992, *Games* magazine ran a contest for palindromes containing famous names. The results were given in the June 1992 issue, with the grand prize awarded to Douglas Fink for "Lisa Bonet ate no basil." Runners-up included, from "A Palindrome Collection" on p. 124, #170 on Noriega and #132 that refers to Finland's Paavo Nurmi, 1920s Olympic track and field medalist. Here are a few more from *Games*, June 1992.

1. Vanna, wanna V?

2. (. . . Yawn.) Madonna fan? No damn way!

3. O, Geronimo: No minor ego!

4. Oh, no! Don Ho!

5. "Is Don Adams mad?" (a nod.) "Sí."

6. "Damn! I, Agassi, miss again! Mad!"

Harpo & Oprah

Here's one by an anonymous writer about the casualties of fame not found in *Games* magazine: "Ed, I saw Harpo Marx ram Oprah W. aside."

Persons Unknown

This palindrome is composed entirely of proper names listed in "A Pronouncing Vocabulary of Common English Given Names" from *Webster's Seventh New Collegiate Dictionary* (1963). It is based on Enavlicm's "Ha, sir, I'm Irish, ah!" and on "Dennis (Krats) and Edna (Stark) sinned," by Evergreen, *TE*, June 1956. The palindrome appears in Dmitri Borgmann's *On Vacation* (1965).

> "Dennis, Nell, Edna, Leon, Nedra, Anita, Rolf, Nora, Alice, Carol, Leo, Jane, Reed, Dena, Dale, Basil, Rae, Penny, Lana, Dave, Denny, Lena, Ida, Bernadette, Ben, Ray, Lila, Nina, Jo, Ira, Mara, Sara, Mario, Jan, Ina, Lily, Arne, Bette, Dan, Reba, Diane, Lynn, Ed, Eva, Dana, Lynne, Pearl, Isabel, Ada, Ned, Dee, Rena, Joel, Lora, Cecil, Aaron, Flora, Tina, Arden, Noel, and Ellen sinned."

Word-Unit Palindromes

A Palindromic Epitaph

A Lyon verse, or Sidonius verse, as it was sometimes called, as a word-unit palindrome, like "The Witch's Prayer," which when read backwards often answers or gives the verse an opposite meaning. Caius Sollius Sidonius Apollinaris, a Gallo-Roman writer from Lyon, France, has been credited with its invention in the fifth century. This example, a sort of epitaph by an unknown author, was probably written in the 1700s or earlier. It was found in St. Winwalloe's churchyard, five miles south of Helston in Cornwall, England. Its words can be read in four directions.

Shall	we	all	die?
We	shall	die	all!
All	die	shall	we?
Die	all	we	shall!

Aphoristic Palindromes

Here is a proverbial word-unit palindrome: "Eat to live; never live to eat." Here are more contemporary examples of word-unit palindromes that make ready aphorisms.

* God knows man. What is doubtful is what man knows God? —*G. J. Blundell*, New Statesman, *ca. 1970*
* Do geese see God? See! Geese do! (The first sentence is a letter-unit palindrome. Combined, the sentences form a word-unit palindrome.)
* All for one and one for all. —*Alexandre Dumas*, The Three Musketeers *(1844)*
* Women understand men; few men understand women. —*Naomi Marks*, New Statesman, *ca. 1970*
* Case development: Arrested suspect calls Doctor Brothers. Doctor calls suspect "arrested development case." —WW, *Nov. 1987, NPL contest*

James A. Lindon's Collection

Here are five palindromes written by James A. Lindon, published in various sources.[1]

* So patient a doctor to doctor a patient so.
* You can cage a swallow, can't you, but you can't swallow a cage, can you?
* Amusing is that company of fond people bores people fond of company that is amusing.

- King, are you glad you are king?
- What! So he is hanged, is he? So what?

Will Shortz & NPR Competition

These winning palindromes come from a competition run by Will Shortz on National Public Radio's "Weekend Edition," Sunday. They were first published in *WW*, Feb. 1997; Shortz wrote: "The quality of the results greatly exceeded my expectations. In fact, some of the submissions might well become new classics." First, the runners-up.

RUNNERS-UP
- Fall leaves after leaves fall. —*Betsy Mirarchi*
- Will my love love my will? —*John Hesemann*
- Please me by standing by me, please! —*Peter Stein*
- Escher, drawing hands, drew hands drawing Escher. —*John Meade*
- Blessed are they that believe that they are blessed. —*Hugh Hazelrigg*
- Says Mom, "What do you do?" You do what Mom says. —*Natalie Heiman*
- You know, I did little for you, for little did I know you. —*Patrick Robbins*
- "Did I say you never say, 'Never say never?' You say I did." —*Bill O'Malley*
- In order to stop hunger, stop to order in. —*Nicole Jabailey*

GRAND PRIZE

The grand prize went to Peter Stein of San Francisco (another of his is quoted above), for this future headline out of Washington, D.C.: "First Ladies Rule the State and State the Rule—'Ladies First!'"

Line-Unit Palindromes

James A. Lindon invented the line-unit palindrome. The original version of Lindon's poem "Doppelgänger" was printed in Dmitri Borgmann's *Beyond Language* (1967). Howard Bergerson in *Palindromes & Anagrams* (1973) presented this revision. The poem reads the same from the first to the last line as it does from the last line to the first.

DOPPELGÄNGER

Entering the lonely house with my wife
I saw him for the first time
Peering furtively from behind a bush—
Blackness that moved,
A shape amid the shadows,
A momentary glimpse of gleaming eyes
Revealed in the ragged moon.
A closer look (he seemed to turn) might have
Put him to flight forever—
I dared not
(For reasons that I failed to understand),
Though I knew I should act at once.

I puzzled over it, hiding alone,
Watching the woman as she neared the gate.
He came, and I saw him crouching
Night after night.
Night after night
He came, and I saw him crouching,
Watching the woman as she neared the gate.

I puzzled over it, hiding alone—
Though I knew I should act at once,
For reasons that I failed to understand
I dared not
Put him to flight forever.

A closer look (he seemed to turn) might have
Revealed in the ragged moon
A momentary glimpse of gleaming eyes,
A shape amid the shadows,
Blackness that moved.

Peering furtively from behind a bush,
I saw him, for the first time,
Entering the lonely house with my wife.

Chapter 16

Word Reversals & Their Pals

Composed in Reverse

This short dictionary of words and couplets will be helpful to those interested in composing palindromes. Archaic and obsolete words are excluded, as are many alternative spellings, foreign and obscure words and names, and localized trade names. I compiled this list with puzzle colleague Kent Aldershof. Dmitri Borgmann's *On Vacation* (1965) and Jeff Grant's *Palindromicon* (1992) are also good sources of palindromic words and word reversals.

You could, of course, cull palindrome collections, like that beginning on p. 100, for appropriate palindromic words. But we've made it easier for you. Here is "A Dictionary of Reversals," and "A Dictionary of One-Word Palindromes" appears on p. 139.

A Dictionary of Reversals

able—Elba
ABM—MBA
abut—tuba
a cap—paca (rodent)
a dad—dada
Adaven (Nevada)—Nevada
ados—soda
a gar—Raga (Sudan)
a garb—Braga (Portugal)
a gem—mega
ages—Sega (trade name)
a goy—yoga
Ah!—Ha!
Ah, Satan!—Natasha
Ailed—Delia

ail Amos—Somalia
aim—MIA, Mia
ajar—Raja, raja
a knot—Tonka (trademark)
Al, al—L.A., la
Allah—halla
Alley—yella
Am—ma
a mal—lama
a Mede—edema
amiced—decima
am Ron—Norma
an—Na, na
an ad—Dana
an aid—Diana
and—DNA
a Ned, an Ed—Dena
a need—Deena
an era—arena
an id—Dina
animal—lamina
a nit—Tina
a nob—bona
an ole crab—Barcelona
an Omar—Ramona
anodes—Sedona (Arizona)
anon—Nona
ante—(Mt.) Etna
a nut—tuna
a pan—Napa (California)
a pap—Papa
a pat—tapa
ape—EPA
a pup—pupa
a rap—para-
are—ERA, era
a repo—opera
ares—sera (plural of *serum*)
a rev—Vera
Ari—IRA, Ira
a roc—Cora

a rod—Dora
a Ron—Nora
array—Yarra (river, Australia)
arret—terra
Aryan—nay, Ra
a sip—Pisa
a slab—balsa
a tad—data
a tram—Marta
a tsar (czar)—Rasta
Avalon—no lava
ave—Eva
avid—diva
Avis—Siva (Shiva)
Avon—Nova, nova
ay—ya
a war at—Tarawa
a yam—Maya
(Francis) Bacon, bacon—no cab
bad—dab
bag—gab
bal—lab
Balder—red Lab (Labrador retriever)
bals—slab
ban—nab
banyan—nay, nab
bar a—Arab
bard—drab
bat—tab
baton—no tab
bats—stab
bed—Deb, deb (Debbie, debutante)
(Brian) Benben (actor)—neb-neb
bid—dib
bin—nib
binder—red nib
bog—gob
bon—nob
bonder—red nob
brag—garb
bro—orb

bros.—Sorb
bud—dub
bun—nub
buns—snub
bur—rub
burg—grub
bus—sub
but—tub
buts—stub
cam—mac
(Albert) Camus—sumac
cap—pac
cares—serac
caw—WAC
cit. (citizen, cited)—tic
cod—doc
cork—(Ray) Kroc
cram—marc
dahs—shad
dam—mad
Damon—nomad
dat—tad
daw—wad
de—Ed
decaf—faced
decal—laced
decap—paced
decider—rediced
dedal—laded
deem—meed
deer—reed
defer—refed
deifier—reified
Deiter—retied
Delbert—trebled
delf—fled
deli—I led
delit—tiled
deliver—reviled
demit—timed
den—Ned

Dennis—sinned
Denton (town)—not Ned
depot—toped
depots—stoped
dessert—tressed
desserts—stressed
detar—rated
devas—saved
devil—lived
dew—wed
dial—laid
dialer—relaid
diaper—repaid
dig—gid
dig rut—turgid
dim—mid
dimit—timid
dine—Enid
dioramas—samaroid
do—od
dog—god
don—nod
doom—mood
door—rood
DOS, dos—sod
draw—ward
drawer—reward
Draw? No.—onward
drawn us—sunward
Draw, oh.—Howard
draws—sward
Draw? Yah.—Hayward
dray—yard
ear—Rae
Edam (city)—made
Edison—no side
edit—tide
eel—Lee, lee
e'en—née
eh?—he
el—le

Elaps—spale
Elbert—treble
Ellen—Nelle
Eliot—toile
em—me
Emil—lime
Emir—rime (alternate spelling)
emit—time
Ergo—ogre
Eris—rise
Eros—sore
Eton—note
Evian (trademark)—naïve
Evan—nave
evil—live
fir—rif
fires—serif
flow—wolf
gal—lag
gals—slag
gar—rag
gas—sag
gat—tag
gateman—name tag
gats—stag
gel—leg
gem—Meg
Gibbons—snob, big
(Bill) Giles—(Bud) Selig
gin—nig (to nidge)
girder—red rig
girt—trig
gnat—tang
gnats—stang (British dialect)
gnaw—Wang
gnus—sung
golf—flog
got—tog
gulp—plug
gum—mug
gums—smug

guns—snug
gut—tug
hahs—shah
Haiku (Hawaii)—Ukiah (California)
hales—selah
har har—rah, rah
Harpo—Oprah
harpoon—No, Oprah.
Harrison—No sir, rah!
haw—wah (panda)
hay—yah
ho—oh
hoop—pooh
I'm, alas—salami
idol—Lodi (town)
I'm—mi
I maim—Miami
I moan—Naomi
Ira's—sari
iron—nori
IRS—sri
is—si
it—Ti, ti
jar—raj
Kay—yak
keel—leek
keels—sleek
keep—peek
knaps—spank
knar—rank
knits—stink
know—wonk
K.O.—O.K.
Kool (trade name)—look
lap—pal
lair—rial
lager—regal
leer—reel
leper—repel
lever—revel
Leon—Noël, noel

liar—rail
lien—Neil
lit—'til
loop—pool
loops—spool
loot—tool
looter—retool
loots—stool
mal—lam
map—Pam
maps—spam, Spam (trade name)
mar—RAM, ram
marcs—scram
mart—tram
Mason, mason—No, Sam.
mat—tam (tam-o'-shanter)
may—yam
meet—teem
Megan—nag 'em
megaton—not a gem
Mets—stem
mho—(George Simon) Ohm, ohm
moor—room
mot—Tom, tom
motmot—tom-tom
murmur—Rum! Rum!
Mustafa (Kemal)—a fat sum
namer—reman
nap—pan
naps—span
nature's—Serutan (trade name)
Nemo—omen
net—ten
nip—pin
nips—spin
nit—tin
nix—X in
no—on
Nola's—salon
no mar—Ramon
no net—tenon

nor—Ron
Norton—not Ron
Norris—sir, Ron
no scut—Tucson (Arizona)
not—ton
no tar—rat on, Raton (New Mexico)
notes—Seton
no tip—piton
not narcs—Scranton (city)
not now—wonton
not sip—piston
now—won
nut—tun
nuts—stun
oat—Tao
os—so
Oy!—Yo!
pacer—recap
pals—slap
pans—snap
par—rap
parcs—scrap
part—trap
parts—strap
pa's—sap
pat—tap
pay—yap
peels—sleep
per—rep
(H. Ross) Perot—to rep
pets—step
pilot—to lip
pins—snip
pit—tip
piton—no tip
(Henri) Pitot, pitot (tube)—to tip
pools—sloop
ports—strop
pot—top
pots—stop
rat—tar

rats—star
raw—war
rebut—tuber
recaps—spacer
red net—tender
red now—wonder
redraw; red, raw—warder
reknit—tinker
reknits—stinker
relit—tiler
remit—timer
repot—toper
rewets—stewer
rot—tor
saps—spas
satraps—Sparta's
saved—Vedas
saw—was
scares—seracs
sew—Wes (Wesley)
Sex? Aw!—waxes
sex is—sixes
sit—'tis
sleets—steels
sloops—spools
smart—trams
smut—Tums (trade name)
snaps—spans
snips—spins
snoops—spoons
snoot—toons
spans—snaps
spat—taps
spay—yaps
spaz—zaps
spit—tips
sports—strops
spot—tops
spots—stops
sprat—tarps
stat—tats

stew—wets
straw—warts
Suez—Zeus
sway—yaws
T. Eliot—toilet
tort—trot
way—yaw

Drop-Letter Reversals

In order to make palindromic phrases, first make reversals of the words in this list by dropping the first or last letter. Dmitri Borgmann calls these *drop-letter reversals*, and wordsmith Chris McManus calls them *embedded reversals*. Borgmann's *Language on Vacation* (1965) supplied these examples. *Pollage* is a rare word for "poll tax," "capitation," or "extortion."

*a*ssauged—degauss
*c*rab-yaws—sway bar
*o*ne myriad—dairymen
*r*egallop—pollage
*r*euniter—retinue
*s*ibilate—et alibi
animativ*e*—vitamin A
dairyma*n*—a myriad
relativ*e*—vitaler
rotativel*y*—levitator

Anchored Reversals

In these *anchored reversals*, created by Dmitri Borgmann in *Language on Vacation* (1965), the first letter in each word or name is dropped.

Catalpa La Plata (Argentina)
Nairobi (Kenya) **c**iboria

In a Word, Singular Palindromes

These single-word palindromes will help you think in reverse and compose pals of your own.

A Dictionary of One-Word Palindromes

ABA / Aba (city) / aba
Abba (music group)
Ada (Ohio and trade name)
aga (agha)
aha
ah-ha
aiaia (aiaiai)
aka / a.k.a.
ala / à la
alla
alula
AMA
amma
ana
anna
anona
Asosa (Ethiopia)
Ava (Missouri)
bib
bob
boob
bub
Capac (Michigan)
civic
dad
deed
degaged
degged (British dialect)
deified
deled
denned
detannated
dewed
did
dud
ecce
Ege (Indiana)
eke
Eleele (Hawaii)

ere
esse
Eve / eve
ewe
Gagag (India)
gag
gig
Glenelg (Maryland, Scotland, Nova Scotia)
hah
hah-hah
Hannah (Michigan and North Dakota)
Harrah (Oklahoma)
huh
Idi (Sumatra, Indonesia)
Ii (river and town, Finland)
Ili (river and district, Russia)
Iliili (American Samoa)
Iki (Island, Japan)
Imi (Ethiopia)
Inini (French Guiana)
Iri (South Korea)
Iriri (river, Brazil)
kaiak (kayak)
Kanak
Kanakanak (Alaska)
Kavak (town in Turkey)
kayak (kaiak)
Kazak
Keek
Kinik (Turkey)
Kinnikinnik
kook
krk (island and town, Yugoslavia)
Kuk (river, Alaska)
La Sal (Utah)
Laval (France and Quebec province)
lavalaval
ma'am
madam
Malayalam
marram

Matam (Senegal)
minim
Mirrim (lake, Uruguay)
mom
mum
Nappan (Nova Scotia)
Nauruan (native of Naura)
Navan (Ireland)
Neuquen (river and town, Argentina)
non
noon
Noxon (Montana); NOXON it reads the same upside down
Noyon (France)
nun
oho
Ohopoho (Zaminia, Africa)
Okonoko (West Virginia)
omo- (shoulder)
Oruro (Bolivia)
Oso (Washington, and river, Zaire)
Otto
Owo (Nigeria)
Oyo (Nigeria)
Oxo (trade name)
pap
peep
pep
pip
pip-pip
poop
pop
pull(-)up
pup
put(-)up
racecar
radar
redder
refer
Reger (Missouri)
reifier
Remer (Minnesota)

Renner (South Dakota and Texas)
repaper
retter
reviver
rotator
rotavator
rotor
sagas
sanas
sayas
Sebes (Romania)
sees
seesees
seities
sememes
semès
Semmes (Alabama)
sesses
sexes
shahs
siris
sis
sisis
Socos (trade name)
solos
SOS
stats
stets
Tahat (mountain, Algeria)
tat
tebet
tenet
terret
Tip-it / Tippit (game)
tit
TNT
Tommot (Russia)
toot
tot
Towot (Sudan)
Tumut (New South Wales, Australia)

Turut (Iran and Turkey)
(King) Tut / tut
tut-tut
Wakaw (Saskatchewan)
Wassamassaw (South Carolina)
Wassaw (sound, Georgia)
Waw-waw (pedal)
wow
Xanax (trade name)
Yessey (Siberia, Russia)
Ziz (Morocco)
zzzz (buzzing or snoring sound)

Call Back

These people's forenames and surnames come in part from collections by Dmitri Borgmann's *Language on Vacation* (1965) and Jeff Grant's *Palindromicon* (1992).

Abba
Ada
Anissina (M., French Olympic ice dancer)
Anna
Asa
Ava
Bab "the Bab," Ali Muhammad of Shiraz (1819–1850), Persian
    religious leader; founder of Bab, also called Babi
Bob
Drakard John, English newspaper proprietor (1775–1854)
Eve
Hannah, forename and surname
Harrah Bill, casino founder; Toby, infielder
Kazak Eddie, infielder
Kerek Angela, German tennis star
Lil short for Lilian and Lillian
Llull Ramon, Catalan mystic and poet (ca. 1235–1316)
Menem Carlos, president of Argentina
Nan; short for Anne and Anna
Nen Robb, pitcher; Dick, first baseman
Odo Eudes, French king, 888–898
Ono Yoko

Otto
Redder Johnny, infielder
Reyer Louis, French composer
Sabas Sylvia, French tennis star
Salas Mark, catcher; a town in Peru
Seles Monica, U.S. tennis star
Soros George, financier
Tenet George, CIA director
Viv or Vyv Vivian
Yy pen name of Robert Lynd, meaning "too wise"

Vertical Palindromes

Identify the palindromic word this verse—found in Rev. Arthur Pearson's *20th Century Standard Puzzle Book* (1907)—suggests.

> A turning point in every day,
> Reversed I do not alter.
> One half of me says haste away!
> The other bids me falter.

The solution is NOON. Other vertical palindromes are the word *dollop*, the trade name OXO, and the autoantonymous phrase "NO X IN NIXON." John M. Culkin calls these *invertograms* and others have called them *vertizontals*.

Vertical Reversal

up dn

Phonetic Pals & Reversals

Here are some phonetic palindromes and reversals. I could add many other examples to both lists. Phonetically palindromic dialogue could be written if enough of these words were found. The phonetic palindrome "top spot" is also a literal or graphic palindrome.

Phonetic Palindromes

crew-work / work-crew
dry yard
easy
Funny enough
Let Bob tell.
new moon
selfless
Sorry, Ross.
Talk, Scott.
to boot
top spot
We revere you.
We taught you.
Y'all lie.
You're caught! Talk, Roy.
You're damn mad, Roy!

Phonetic Reversals

Bach / bock—cob
back(s)—(s)cab
bar—rob
boar / bore—robe
buck—cub
butt(s)—(s)tub
cap—pack
(s)coops—spook(s)
crawl—lark
cup—Puck / puck
ether—earthy (antonymous)
feel—life
fleshpot—topshelf (transposal)
fox—scoff
play—yelp
pore—rope
(s)crew—work(s)
tart—trot
we—you

In Reverse

- BOSS in reverse reads SSOB (double S.O.B.).
- STROHS ON TAP, reading backwards, spells "Pat no shorts."
- EMBARGO—"O grab me!" (which reads palindromically "Embargo, go grab me!") was the nickname given to Thomas Jefferson's Embargo Act of 1808, because of the many who flagrantly violated it.
- EVIAN, the name of a bottled water, is a reversal of "naïve."
- In 1968, STEVIE WONDER recorded under the anonym of Eivets Rednow, presumably to avoid a breach of contract suit by Motown Records.
- Fashion designer Arnold ISAACS found that his last name in reverse, Scaasi, spells success.
- The surname MAHARG is Graham spelled backwards (probably "gray home" in Old English). One story has it that during a British dispute the name was reversed to protect those named Graham from persecution.
- The name Yokum is a phonetic reversal of MCCOY.
- Baseball commissioner Bud SELIG's name is a reversal of Bill GILES, president of the Philadelphia Phillies.

Words Reconsidered

LIVE ON REVILED reads backwards as "Deliver no evil." By inserting "sides reversed is" between the two phrases (a trick devised by Leigh Mercer in 1946), it forms the palindrome "'Deliver no evil,' sides reversed, is 'Live on reviled.'"

Another type of reversal is a sentence that can be read in both directions word by word, but which is not palindromic. Consider these century-old examples: "Scandalous society and life make gossips frantic." Or, "Frantic gossips make life and society scandalous."

Chapter 17

Word Squares & Crosswords

Form Puzzles & Early Crosswords

Form puzzles, such as word diamonds and squares, were predecessors of the *crossword*. More closely related to the crossword are the difficult and rare double forms, in which vertical and horizontal words differ. In an ordinary word square, each word runs in both directions, like the word *scar* in the first row and first column of H.E.P.'s word square above. Because a form puzzle contains no black squares, it requires more skill to construct than a crossword. Forms and crosswords are certainly more difficult to build than to solve.

These word squares by H. E. P. (probably Harriet Eleanor Phillimon) appeared in the London journal *N&Q* July 16, 1859.

WORD SQUARES
H. E. P. (1859)

```
S  C  A  R        A  I  S  L  E
C  U  B  E        I  D  I  O  M
A  B  L  E        S  I  E  V  E
R  E  E  L        L  O  V  E  R
                  E  M  E  R  Y


C  R  E  W        C  R  E  S  T
R  A  V  E        R  E  A  C  H
E  V  E  R        E  A  G  E  R
W  E  R  E        S  C  E  N  E
                  T  H  R  E  E


J  U  S  T        M  I  G  H  T
U  G  L  Y        I  D  L  E  R
S  L  I  P        G  U  I  D  E
T  Y  P  E        H  E  D  G  E
                  T  R  E  E  S
```

Arthur Wynne originated the first crossword as we know it, then called a *word-cross*, published in the *New York World* Sunday supplement, Dec. 21, 1913. The first book of crosswords published in America appeared Apr. 10, 1924. In 1925, British newspapers adopted the American crossword, which developed a more difficult style of its own, and *les mots croisés* began appearing in France.

Constructing Word Squares

In making a word square or form puzzle, words with alternating vowels and consonants are the easiest to build on. The more consonants in the words, especially in the bottom row, the more difficult it is to create. The letters *Q, J, X, V,* and *Z* are especially challenging to the form-builder. When composing or solving a large form puzzle, at least a large dictionary and a gazetteer or atlas are essential.

Although there are no established rules in form-building, many puzzlers advise against using proper name and abbreviations not listed in standard references. A perfect form puzzle, in my view, contains no slang words, phrases, or terms that are hyphenated, rare, archaic, obsolete, regional, or strictly foreign.

Although phrases and nondictionary words are acceptable to many formists, very few are shown in the forms in this book. Many examples included here are composed of current common words.

According to puzzle historian Theodore G. Meyer, the earliest-known word square in English uses just three words, "cat ate tea." It appeared in the early 1850s in "a little volume published for the curious."

C A T
A T E
T E A

Four-Word Squares

In 1860 the *American Almanac* featured a palindromic four-word square containing three English words, *time, item,* and *emit.* According Dr. Joseph Emerson Worcester in *The Geographical Dictionary* (1817), *Meti,* the fourth word, was the name of a town in Abyssinia (now Ethiopia).

The earliest-known palindromic word square published in America which contained no foreign words was by Nellie Jay (Nellie Jones) found in "Round the Evening Lamp," in the Boston magazine *Our Young Folks*, May 1871.

Palindromic Four-Word Squares

(1860)

```
T  I  M  E
I  T  E  M
M  E  T  I
E  M  I  T
```

Nellie Jay (1871)

```
S  T  E  W
T  I  D  E
E  D  I  T
W  E  T  S
```

Five-Word Squares

An anonymous contributor to *N&Q* Sept. 3, 1859, provided a word square we've titled "Warning," which reads across and down: "Leave Ellen alone, venom enemy!" Compare this with the word square on p. 147 that could be read as a complete sentence: "Might idler glide hedge trees?" The puzzler states: "The conclusion to be drawn from exercises of this kind is that four letters are nothing at all; that five letters are so easy that nothing is worth notice unless the combination has meaning. Six letters, done in any way, are respectable, and seven letters would be a triumph. I have seen only one combination of five letters with meaning, as follows, given me by the friend who made it."

WARNING
(1859)

```
L  E  A  V  E
E  L  L  E  N
A  L  O  N  E
V  E  N  O  M
E  N  E  M  Y
```

Charlie B. composed the first America-made five-word square ("Light-Trent") published. It appeared in the "Headwork" column of *Our Boys & Girls*, also called *Oliver Optic's Magazine*, Feb. 1, 1868. It is similar to the five-word square "Might idler glide hedge trees?" on p. 147. Oliver Optic was the pseudonym of the magazine's editor, William Taylor Adams (1822–1897), father of puzzledom and noted story writer for young readers. Imperial made the first double word square, printed in the Toledo, Ohio, magazine, *Our Boys*, Feb. 1, 1871.

What we call word squares today were called both "word squares" and "square words" until the term *word square* was officially defined in the 1879 *Supplement to Webster's Unabridged Dictionary*: "a series of words so arranged that they can be read vertically and horizontally with the like result" resembling that shown below.

Earliest American

FIVE-WORD SQUARE
Charlie B. (1868)
L I G H T
I D L E R
G L A R E
H E R O N
T R E N T

WEBSTER'S 1879 EXAMPLE
H E A R T
E M B E R
A B U S E
R E S I N
T R E N T

FIRST DOUBLE-WORD SQUARE
Imperial (1871)
T E R M
A L O E
P L A T
S A M E

Double Five-Word Square

Niagara made the first double five-word square found in *Our Boys & Girls*, Feb. 1875.

DOUBLE FIVE-WORD SQUARE
Niagara (1875)
```
S T A M P
M A L A R
A P O D E
R I N G S
T R E E S
```

Palindromes & Cryptograms

This palindromic cryptogrammatic five-word square by Skeeziks was found in the column "Puzzledom" in *Golden Days*, Dec. 3, 1884.

PALINDROMIC CRYPTOGRAM
Skeeziks (1884)
```
3 2 1 2 3       L A S A L
2 5 4 5 2       A N O N A
1 4 3 4 1       S O L O S
2 5 4 5 2       A N O N A
3 2 1 2 3       L A S A L
```

The crypt solution is the word *salon*.

Polyglot Word Squares

Here are some polyglot word squares. The first one, "Polyglot" by D.C. Ver, appeared in *Ardmore Puzzler*, Jan. 15, 1907, and the second one, a ten-language double word square, was created by Chris Long on a computer in 1992.

In the five-word square titled "Polyglot," the word *damen* is German; *amico*, Italian; *mitos*, Greek; *école*, French; and *noses*, English.

POLYGLOT
D. C. Ver (1907)

```
D A M E N
A M I C O
M I T O S
E C O L E
N O S E S
```

The computer-made double-word square boasts these words and ten languages: (across) *aagje*, Dutch; *falot*, French; *flirt*, English; *yttra*, Swedish; *rotol*, Italian; (down) *affyr*, Danish; *aalto*, Finnish; *glitt*, German; *jorro*, Spanish; and *ettal*, Norwegian.

POLYGLOT DOUBLE
Chris Long & Computer (1992)

```
A A G J E
F A L O T
F L I R T
Y T T R A
R O T O L
```

Connected Squares

To complicate puzzle construction still more, here are three five-word squares neatly connected to create a single form puzzle. "Connected Squares" was created by the puzzler Pedestrian for the *Danbury News* column "Witch Knots," May 13, 1876.

CONNECTED SQUARES
Pedestrian (1876)

```
            J U D E A
            U S I N G
            D I V A N
            E N A T E
C H A M P A G N E S U P P E R
H O N O R     P O L K A
A N I M A     P L A I N
M O M U S     E K I N G
P R A S E     R A N G E
```

Six-Word Squares

Circle & Square Squared

The first six-word square here, "Circle Squared," that begins with the word *circle* and ends with the word *esteem*, was first published in *N&Q*, July 2, 1859 and later in *Wilkes' Spirit of the Times*, Sept. 2, 1859. The second "improved" version omits the proper name Icarus and substitutes four new words (*inures*, *rudest*, *crease*, and *lessee*) for the former four middle words (*Icarus*, *rarest*, *create*, and *lustre*). The second version appeared in Dmitri Borgmann's *Language on Vacation* (1965). And then we have Dmitri Borgmann's "Square Squared," published in *Newsweek*, Nov. 2, 1964.

CIRCLE SQUARED (1859)

```
C I R C L E
I C A R U S
R A R E S T
C R E A T E
L U S T R E
E S T E E M
```

"IMPROVED" CIRCLE SQUARED (1965)

```
C I R C L E
I N U R E S
R U D E S T
C R E A S E
L E S S E E
E S T E E M
```

SQUARE SQUARED
Dmitri Borgmann (1964)

```
S Q U A R E
Q I N T A R
U N L A C E
A T A V I C
R A C I S T
E R E C T S
```

Our Young Folks Challenge

A. Langdon Root composed the first American-made six-word square, published in *Our Young Folks* magazine, Mar. 1871. The readers were given the first two words, *scions* and *catnip*, and offered the challenge of finding the other four. Of the 28 puzzlers who responded, eleven completed it. Here is the solution.

SIX-WORD CHALLENGE
(1871)

```
S  C  I  O  N  S
C  A  T  N  I  P
I  T  H  A  C  A
O  N  A  G  E  R
N  I  C  E  S  T
S  P  A  R  T  A
```

Several contributors formed another word square in which NICENE replaced NICEST, and SPARED, SPARES, AND SPARER replaced SPARTA. Hitty Maginn stated in the Feb. 1871 issue that he made more than 100 attempts at a six-word square. In the four months following the published solution, the magazine received over two dozen six-word squares from readers. In the June issue, the editors challenged readers with a seven-word square, but results were disappointing.

Word Cubes

Still Six Abreast

Jeff in *WW*, Aug. 1978, presented these six interrelated six-word cubes. All words are from the *OED*. Each boldface letter in the upper left corner of each word cube, taken together, spells the word REMADE. Also, each of the original words from the first cube becomes the first row and first column of the succeeding cube. So, the word *enamel* heads the second cube, *macula* the third, *amulet* the fourth, *delete* the fifth, and *elater* the sixth. Also note the diagonal repetition of the word *ere* in the sixth cube.

You can also read across all six cubes. Start, for instance, with the second row of each, and read across "enamel, narine, arenas, minime, enamor, and lesere." If you read down the second cube, you will find the same words repeated. This works for all six rows, the third row matching the third cube, etc., just as all words (save the first word) from the first cube head succeeding cubes.

```
R E M A D E        E N A M E L        M A C U L A
E N A M E L        N A R I N E        A R E N A S
M A C U L A        A R E N A S        C E R I T E
A M U L E T        M I N I M E        U N I T E R
D E L E T E        E N A M O R        L A T E R E
E L A T E R        L E S E R E        A S E R E D

A M U L E T        D E L E T E        E L A T E R
M I N I M E        E N A M O R        L E S E R E
U N I T E R        L A T E R E        A S E R E D
L I T O T E        E M E T I N        T E R E N E
E M E T I N        T O R I E D        E R E N D E
T E R E N E        E R E N D E        R E D E E M
```

Windmill

Walter Shedlofsky in *WW*, Aug. 1973, provided this windmill of a six-word square.

```
E S C A R P
S I E V E R
C E R I S E
A V I S O S
R E S O R T
P R E S T I S  S I  M O
       S  O  O N  E R
       S  O  R T  E D
       I  N  T A  K E
       M  E  E K  E R
       O  R  D E  R S
```

Word Square with Rhymed Verse Clues

The first word square printed with clues in rhymed verse was this six-word square by puzzler S. E. G. in *Our Young Folks*, May 1871.

WORD-SQUARE PUZZLE
S. E. G. (1871)

Without my first, naught can be made.
My second, we wish our friends to do.
To sit on my third, I am afraid.
Some love my fourth, alas! 'Tis true.
To see my fifth, we watch the flowers,
And for my last, ask heavenly powers.

```
M A T T E R
A R R I V E
T R I P O D
T I P P L E
E V O L V E
R E D E E M
```

Double Six-Word Squares

The puzzler Rose Budd is credited with making the first double six-word square, printed in *Danbury News*, summer 1876. But Gil Blas created the first widely-recognized example in *Wild Oats*, Aug. 22, 1878.

DOUBLE SIX-WORD SQUARE
Gil Blas (1878)
```
P A N A D A
O B E L U S
M A C L E S
A T T U N E
D E O D A R
E R N E S T
```

Exceptional Double Six-Word Squares

The words used in these double six-word squares can be found in most unabridged dictionaries. The first two squares contain most common words. The first is by Eric, published in *TE*, Dec. 1990, and the second by M. D(ouglas). McIlroy, published in *WW*, 1976, was computer-made. The third and fourth double word-squares were also computer-made by Chris Long in 1992. The words in these last two double word-squares can be found in the unabridged second edition of *Webster's New International Dictionary* (1960). The letters *X* and *J* in the top and bottom words of the fourth word-square are difficult to use in form-building.

DOUBLE SIX-WORD SQUARES
Eric (1990)

```
A  S  S  E  T  S
S  C  H  L  E  P
T  H  R  A  L  L
H  O  O  P  L  A
M  O  U  S  E  Y
A  L  D  E  R  S
```

M. D. McIlroy & Computer (1976)

```
S  C  H  I  S  T
P  R  I  N  C  E
R  A  T  T  O  N
I  N  T  E  N  D
T  I  E  R  C  E
E  A  R  N  E  R
```

Chris Long & Computer (1992)

```
S  Q  U  A  R  E
T  U  N  N  E  R
R  O  S  O  L  I
Y  T  T  R  I  C
C  H  O  A  N  A
H  A  W  K  E  D
```

Chris Long & Computer (1992)

```
S  C  O  L  E  X
W  I  R  I  L  Y
A  N  A  N  A  S
R  E  C  E  N  T
A  N  L  A  C  E
J  E  E  R  E  R
```

Progressive Word Squares

The puzzler Sphinx made the first progressive word square, published in *Wild Oats*, Oct. 8, 1876. In the progressive word square, the second letter of each word begins the word in the succeeding line. The earliest progressive six-word square was by puzzlers Ben J. Min and Comet. The two puzzle-makers independently submitted the same word combination to Hal Hazard, editor of "Marginalia" in the newspaper *Baltimore Item*. The progressive six-word square was published Mar. 19, 1881.

PROGRESSIVE SIX-WORD SQUARE
Ben J. Min and Comet (1881)

```
R E L A T E
E L A T E S
L A T E S T
A T E S T E
T E S T E R
E S T E R S
```

Seven-Word Squares

First Seven

The first seven-word square appeared by Skeeziks in *Wild Oats*, June 27, 1877. Here are glosses on some of the words in the seven-word square: *Camargo* is a town in Bolivia, and the word *osselet* means "a small bone, such as one of the three in the ear's tympanic cavity."

Skeeziks (1877)

```
C A M A R G O
A T O N E R S
M O T I V E S
A N I L I N E
R E V I V A L
G R E N A D E
O S S E L E T
```

Magnificent Sevens

These seven-word squares (1 to 8) contain no phrases, no proper names, and no obsolete, rare, archaic, or hyphenated words. (1) The first seven-word square in our collection is by puzzler Hal Hazard; it appeared in "Puzzle Calls" in the *Newark Sunday Call*, May 6, 1888. (2) The second is a later version of a word square composed by William Fenwick, of the British Puzzlers' League, found in "Our Puzzle Column," the *Henry Republican* of Aug. 17, 1882. The first and second words in the original were *targets* and *avernat* (*avernal* is more familiar), and the sixth word was *stayers*. (3) A. F. Holt created this seven-word square, published in the *Henry Republican*, May 1, 1884. It uses the British spelling *sceptre*. (4, 5) These two seven-word squares are from a set of 15 by puzzler Simon Ease from July 3, 1884 *Henry Republican*. (6, 7) These two seven-word squares were made by Chris Long on a computer in 1992. (8) Dmitri Borgmann said this seven-word square was the best square he had seen of this size. It was computer-generated by M. D. McIlroy, *WW*, Nov. 1975.

1. Hal Hazard (1888)

P R E P A R E
R E M O D E L
E M U L A T E
P O L E M I C
A D A M A N T
R E T I N U E
E L E C T E D

2. William Fenwick (1882)

M E R G E R S
E T E R N A L
R E G A T T A
G R A V I T Y
E N T I T L E
R A T T L E R
S L A Y E R S

3. A. F. Holt (1884)

```
R  O  A  S  T  E  R
O  B  S  C  E  N  E
A  S  S  E  R  T  S
S  C  E  P  T  R  E
T  E  R  T  I  A  N
E  N  T  R  A  N  T
R  E  S  E  N  T  S
```

4. Simon Ease (1884)

```
I  M  P  A  S  T  O
M  O  U  N  T  E  D
P  U  R  G  E  R  Y
A  N  G  L  E  R  S
S  T  E  E  V  E  S
T  E  R  R  E  N  E
O  D  Y  S  S  E  Y
```

5. Simon Ease (1884)

```
N  E  S  T  L  E  S
E  N  T  R  A  N  T
S  T  R  A  N  G  E
T  R  A  I  T  O  R
L  A  N  T  E  R  N
E  N  G  O  R  G  E
S  T  E  R  N  E  R
```

6. Chris Long & Computer (1992)

```
V  I  S  C  E  R  A
I  M  P  A  N  E  L
S  P  I  T  T  L  E
C  A  T  E  R  E  R
E  N  T  R  E  A  T
R  E  L  E  A  S  E
A  L  E  R  T  E  D
```

7. Chris Long & Computer (1992)

```
M A C A B R E
A M A T E U R
C A N T A T A
A T T E S T S
B E A S T I E
R U T T I E R
E R A S E R S
```

8. M. D. McIlroy (1975)

```
W A S S A I L
A N T E N N A
S T R I N G Y
S E I Z U R E
A N N U L A R
I N G R A T E
L A Y E R E D
```

Seven Up

According to Sherlock Holmes, master word-square and form builder, it is ten times more difficult to build an eight-word square than a seven-word square, and ten times as hard to compose a nine-word square than an eight-word square. A double eight-word square has been thought to be as difficult to compose as the nine-word square.

The first double seven-word and eight-word squares contained very obscure words, as did the first regular nine-word square, shown here.

Chris Long's computer-made double seven-word square from 1992 is the best "double seven" I've seen. It contains no proper nouns and all words are in Webster's second unabridged dictionary.

Sherlock Holmes, at age seventy, produced, without computer assistance, what I consider the second best double seven-word square, published in *TE*, Aug. 1972, and shown on the following page. His word square contains no proper nouns, and eleven words are found in Webster's second unabridged dictionary, including *vincent* (rare), meaning "victorious."

Mattie Jay published the first double seven-word square in the "Salmagundi" column of the *Baltimore Sunday News*, Oct. 19, 1882.

FIRST DOUBLE SEVEN-WORD SQUARE
Mattie Jay (1882)

```
C  A  R  A  M  A  N
A  L  A  M  O  D  E
R  A  V  E  L  E  D
A  T  E  L  E  N  E
B  E  N  I  S  O  N
A  R  E  N  O  S  E
S  E  R  E  N  E  S
```


"BEST" DOUBLE SEVEN-WORD SQUARE
Chris Long & Computer (1992)

```
S  MA  S  H  E  S
P  ON  T  I  N  E
I  NG  R  A  T  E
R  EL  A  T  E  R
A  SI  N  I  N  E
L  IN  G  O  T  S
S  AG  E  N  E  S
```


DOUBLE SEVEN-WORD SQUARE
Sherlock Holmes (1972)

```
M  A  R  A  R  I  E
I  D  O  L  I  N  G
S  E  M  E  N  C  E
A  L  A  R  G  E  S
V  I  N  C  E  N  T
E  N  C  E  N  S  E
R  E  E  S  T  E  D
```

Eight-Word Squares

Eights First

Dona Telore, who edited the monthly journal *Fairmount Puzzler*, built the first eight-word square on June 18, 1884 and published it July 31, 1884. He composed it nearly a month and a half before an identical square was published under the pseudonyms C. U. Rious and Will Dexter. Use of the same combination of words was coincidental. Dona Telore explained that he had not printed his word square sooner because he wanted to sell it, but had not received a suitable offer.

About two weeks before he claimed to have composed his eight-word square, *Newark Puzzler* editor Adonis showed at least three of his own to other formists. Each of his word squares was missing one letter. C. U. Rious—after reading Dona Telore's claim that he made an eight-word square, but not seeing Telore's word square or that by Adonis (below)—submitted his nearly finished square to Will Dexter. Dexter finished it with four letters, by using a larger dictionary.

FIRST EIGHT-WORD SQUARE
Dona Telore (1884)

```
G A D A W A R A
A N E L A C E S
D E T A S T E S
A L A N T I N E
W A S T I N G S
A C T I N I A S
R E E N G A G E
A S S E S S E D
```

EIGHT-WORD SQUARE
Adonis (1884)

```
_ R A G T A R A
R E T R A C E S
A T L A N T E S
G R A P L I N E
T A N L I N G S
A C T I N I A S
R E E N G A G E
A S S E S S E D
```

EIGHT-WORD SQUARE
C. U. Rious (1884)

```
P  A  R  A  P  A  R  A
A  N  E  L  A  C  E  S
R  E     A  S  T  E  S
L  A  N  T  I  N  E  A
P  A  S  T  I  N  G  S
A  C  T  I  N  I  A  S
R  E  E  N  G  A  G  E
A  S  S  E  S  S  E  D
```

Simon Ease made the second eight-word square to be published; it appeared Sept. 13, 1884 in "Our Puzzle Column," *Henry Republican*. Jarep, the first puzzler to compile a word list for building forms, showed Bolis how, by altering two words, the geographical name *Tergeste* could be eliminated in the word square. *Tergeste* is replaced with *turgesce* and the second word *Atlantes* with *ailantus*. That left only two objectionable words, *Baptista*, a character from Shakespeare's *Taming of the Shrew* (1593), and *Tanninge*, another geographical name. Jarep and Bolis's revised eight-word square appeared in *Newark Puzzler*, Oct. 1884.

EIGHT-WORD SQUARE
Simon Ease (1884)

```
B  A  P  T  I  S  T  A
A  T  L  A  N  T  E  S
P  L  U  N  D  E  R  S
T  A  N  N  I  N  G  E
I  N  D  I  C  T  E  R
S  T  E  N  T  E  S  T
T  E  R  G  E  S  T  E
A  S  S  E  R  T  E  D
```

REVISED EIGHT-WORD SQUARE
Jarep & Bolis (1884)

```
B  A  P  T  I  S  T  A
A  I  L  A  N  T  U  S
P  L  U  N  D  E  R  S
T  A  N  N  I  N  G  E
I  N  D  I  C  T  E  R
S  T  E  N  T  E  S  T
T  U  R  G  E  S  C  E
A  S  S  E  R  T  E  D
```

Eric Albert composed the "Best Eight-Word Square" on a computer. (See below.) All of its words are in Webster's second unabridged dictionary, except *pimenton*, which appears in *Webster's New World Dictionary*, third college edition. Margaretta Strohm built the "'Second Best' Eight-Word Square" without computer aid. The original word in the sixth position was *cantoral*, according to *TE*, Nov. 1926.

BEST EIGHT-WORD SQUARE
Eric Albert & Computer (1989)

```
O  P  A  L  E  S  C  E
P  I  M  E  N  T  O  N
A  M  E  N  D  I  N  G
L  E  N  T  A  N  D  O
E  N  D  A  N  G  E  R
S  T  I  N  G  I  N  G
C  O  N  D  E  N  S  E
E  N  G  O  R  G  E  D
```

"SECOND BEST" EIGHT-WORD SQUARE
Margaretta Strohm (1926)

```
A  G  A  R  I  C  U  S
G  E  N  E  R  A  N  T
A  N  A  C  O  N  D  A
R  E  C  A  N  T  E  R
I  R  O  N  W  O  R  T
C  A  N  T  O  N  A  L
U  N  D  E  R  A  G  E
S  T  A  R  T  L  E  D
```

Tunste made the first double eight-word square, published in *Daily Inter-Ocean*, Oct. 15, 1901.

The "Q" Eight-Word Square, computer-made by Chris Long, is the only one of its size.

The Connected Double Eight-Word Square, which he also discovered, is the only one composed entirely of words in Merriam-Webster's dictionaries. He crated both the "Q" and the connected word squares in 1992.

FIRST DOUBLE EIGHT-WORD SQUARE
Tunste (1901)

```
F  A  T  A  L  I  S  M
A  M  A  R  A  N  T  A
T  A  L  E  N  G  E  S
A  R  E  S  T  E  R  S
L  A  N  T  E  N  N  E
I  N  T  E  R  N  A  T
S  T  E  N  N  E  T  T
T  E  S  S  E  R  A  E
```

"Q" EIGHT-WORD SQUARE
Chris Long & Computer (1992)

```
Q  U  A  D  R  I  A  D
U  N  T  R  A  N  C  E
A  T  L  A  N  T  I  C
D  R  A  I  S  I  N  E
R  A  N  S  O  M  E  D
I  N  T  I  M  A  T  E
A  C  I  N  E  T  A  N
D  E  C  E  D  E  N  T
```

CONNECTED DOUBLE EIGHT-WORD SQUARES
Chris Long & Computer (1992)

```
C  A  I  M  A  C  A  M  E  S  D  A  M  E  S
A  G  M  I  N  A  T  E  X  P  I  R  A  N  T
I  M  P  L  A  N  T  S  P  R  A  T  T  L  E
M  I  L  K  M  A  I  D  I  A  M  E  T  E  R
A  N  A  M  I  R  T  A  R  T  E  S  I  A  N
C  A  N  A  R  I  U  M  A  T  T  I  N  G  S
A  T  T  I  T  U  D  E  N  L  E  A  G  U  E
M  E  S  D  A  M  E  S  T  E  R  N  S  E  T
```

Here are two more eight-word squares found by Chris Long's computer search in 1992. Richard Sabey created the final eight-word square with computer aid and words from *Webster's Third New International Dictionary*, unabridged (1971). Sabey's word square was published in *WW*, Aug. 1995.

MORE EIGHT-WORD SQUARES
Chris Long & Computer (1992)

```
B  I  G  A  M  I  S  T
I  M  A  G  I  N  E  R
G  A  M  E  S  O  M  E
A  G  E  N  E  S  I  S
M  I  S  E  D  I  T  S
I  N  O  S  I  T  O  L
S  E  M  I  T  O  N  E
T  R  E  S  S  L  E  T
```

Chris Long & Computer (1992)

```
B  E  C  L  A  S  P  S
E  P  H  E  M  E  R  A
C  H  A  P  E  R  O  N
L  E  P  O  R  I  N  E
A  M  E  R  I  C  A  N
S  E  R  I  C  A  T  E
P  R  O  N  A  T  E  S
S  A  N  E  N  E  S  S
```

Richard Sabey (1995)

```
N  E  A  T  H  E  R  D
E  N  G  R  A  V  E  R
A  G  M  I  N  A  T  E
T  R  I  N  D  L  E  S
H  A  N  D  G  U  N  S
E  V  A  L  U  A  T  E
R  E  T  E  N  T  O  R
D  R  E  S  S  E  R  S
```

Nine-Word Squares

Quaint Wonders Here

Arthur F. Holt made the first nine-word square, which appeared as puzzle #10,000 in the Chicago *Sunday Inter-Ocean*, Dec. 28, 1897. Better nine-word squares by Holt and others were published soon thereafter. The *Ardmore Puzzler*, Nov. 15, 1904, featured ten of Holt's nine-word squares. Hercules composed the anagram THE NINE-WORD SQUARE—"quaint wonders here," which says it all.

Clues to the second nine-word square shown below were given in *TE*, Sept. 1992. It was computer-generated by Chris Long, who published it, his first word square, under the NPL pseudonym Cubist. It is composed of unhyphenated lowercase dictionary words, all but one of which (*trabeatae*), are in the *OED*.

FIRST NINE-WORD SQUARE
Arthur Holt (1897)

```
Q U A R E L E S T
U P P E R E S T E
A P P O I N T E R
R E O M E T E R S
E R I E V I L L E
L E N T I L L I N
E S T E L L I N E
S T E R L I N G S
T E R S E N E S S
```

COMPUTER-MADE NINE-WORD SQUARES
Chris Long & Computer (1992)

```
B O R T S C H E S
O V E R T R U S T
R E P A R E N C E
T R A B E A T A E
S T R E S T E L L
C R E A T U R A L
H U N T E R I T E
E S C A L A T E S
S T E E L L E S S
```

Chris Long & Computer (1992)

```
V  E  S  P  A  C  I  D  E
E  C  H  O  L  A  L  I  A
S  H  E  E  T  L  E  S  S
P  O  E  T  I  C  I  S  E
A  L  T  I  M  E  T  E  R
C  A  L  C  E  V  I  V  E
I  L  E  I  T  I  S  E  S
D  I  S  S  E  V  E  R  S
E  A  S  E  R  E  S  S  E
```

More Nines

The nine-word square based on *mergences* was crated by Eric Albert and his computer. It was the first nine-word square composed entirely of words from one source, Webster's second unabridged dictionary. Most formists believed that such a square would be impossible. It could be said that its only (minor) flaws are the capitalized word *Sturnidae* and the obsolete word *circumfer*. *WW*, Nov. 1991, featured an interesting article by Mr. Albert, a computer scientist and noted crossword constructor, on how he developed his program to find the square in June 1989.

On the following page are two more squares made by Chris Long with his trusty computer. Every word in the "Reedlesse" square is in the *OED*. This was the second nine-word square made of words from a single source, published in *TE*, Sept. 1993

Although the "Serenesse"-based word square from *TE*, Feb. 1993 contains a hyphenated word, it also has two Xs, two Zs, and three Ks—letters difficult to use in any word square or form. Remarkably, six words in this nine-word square contain at least one of these difficult letters. All words can be found in Webster's second unabridged dictionary, except *karatekas*, from *Chambers Dictionary* (1994), which means "karate experts," and *epoxidize* from the unabridged *Webster's Third New International Dictionary* (1971) and the *OED*. All three are excellent examples of nine-word squares.

SINGLE-SOURCE NINES
Eric Albert & Computer (1991)

```
N E C E S S I S M
E X I S T E N C E
C I R C U M F E R
E S C A R P I N G
S T U R N I D A E
S E M P I T E R N
I N F I D E L I C
S C E N A R I Z E
M E R G E N C E S
```

STILL NINE WORDS
Chris Long & Computer (1992)

```
W O R C E S T E R
O V E R L A R G E
R E C O I N A G E
C R O S S T I E D
E L I S I O N A L
S A N T O N A T E
T R A I N A G E S
E G G E A T E R S
R E E D L E S S E
```

```
K A R A T E K A S
A P O C O P A T E
R O S E C O L O R
A C E T O X I M E
T O C O K I N I N
E P O X I D I Z E
K A L I N I T E S
A T O M I Z E R S
S E R E N E S S E
```

Ten-Word Squares

A. F. Holt built the first ten-word square, shown here in slightly modified form, published in *TE*, Dec. 1921. It was composed entirely of tautonyms and based on a technique conceived by Tunste a year earlier. In the original square, the word *orang-utang* was originally *arangarang* and the word *tangatanga* was originally *rangaranga*. Gyles Brandreth of *Joy of Lex* (1980) discusses definitions and sources.

TAUTONYMIC "TEN"
A. F. Holt (1921)

```
O  R  A  N  G  U  T  A  N  G
R  A  N  G  A  R  A  N  G  A
A  N  D  O  L  A  N  D  O  L
N  G  O  T  A  N  G  O  T  A
G  A  L  A  N  G  A  L  A  N
U  R  A  N  G  U  T  A  N  G
T  A  N  G  A  T  A  N  G  A
A  N  D  O  L  A  N  D  O  L
N  G  O  T  A  N  G  O  T  A
G  A  L  A  N  G  A  L  A  N
```

Top Ten & Double Nine

Words Ways has published ten-word squares without tautonyms. Jeff Grant created ten-word squares, each containing at least one word not listed in a standard reference. Recent work by Eric Albert, Chris Long, and Jeff Grant suggests that an all-dictionary ten-word square might eventually be composed, but according to Palmer Peterson, "the chance of a genuine" double nine-word square is "nil." Chris Long has written articles on square-building in *WW*, Feb. 1993 and May 1993 issues.

Key to Abbreviations

Here are shortened book titles; abbreviations for periodicals; notes about popular puzzle columns, editors, and organizations; and some other important sources for this book. Many other books, articles, magazines, newspapers, and broadsides were consulted. These "short lists" will help you identify attributed puzzlemakers and enjoy word puzzle history.

Shortened Book Titles

A Key to Puzzledom William W. Delaney, et al., *A Key to Puzzledom; or Complete Handbook of the Enigmatic Art* (1906); published by William W. Delaney for EPL

Alphabet Avenue David Morice, *Alphabet Avenue: Life in the Fast Lane* (1997)

"Anagrammasia" Amaranth (Newton B. Lovejoy), "Anagrammasia," unpublished book manuscript (1926) shared by NPL members

An Almanac Willard R. Espy, *An Almanac of Words at Play* (1975)

Another Almanac Willard R. Espy, *Another Almanac of Words at Play* (1980)

Ballou's Monthly Magazine William Clarke, *Ballou's Monthly Magazine*; Boston; column "Ruthven's Puzzle Page," edited by Ruthven (Edwin R. Briggs, 1872–1891)

Beyond Language Dmitri A. Borgmann, *Beyond Language: Adventures in Word & Thought* (1967)

Daffodil John Pool, *Lid off a Daffodil* (1982)

Devil's Dictionary Ambrose Gwinett Bierce, *The Devil's Dictionary* (1911)

Dynamos Jon Agee, *So Many Dynamos! (& Other Palindromes)* (1994)

1893 Puzzlers' Directory Ernest W. Ager, *The "1893" Puzzlers' Directory*

Enigma Puzzlers' Directory *The Enigma Puzzlers' Directory* (1927); directories issued annually by the National Puzzlers' League

From A to Zotamorf Stephen J. Chism, *From A to Zotamorf: The Dictionary of Palindromes; Word Ways* monograph series no. 4 (1992)

Gleanings (1860) Charles Carroll Bombaugh, *Gleanings from the Harvest Fields of Literature, Science & Art* (1860) This was the first book of word recreations published in the United States. Since 1860, there have been many revisions and new editions, some with title changes, notably 1867, 1870, 1875, and 1890; it was also reissued and updated as *Oddities & Curiosities* (1961), edited with annotations by Martin Gardner.

Gleanings (1867) Charles Carroll Bombaugh, *Gleanings from the Harvest Fields of Literature*, 3rd edition (1867)

Go Hang Jon Agee, *Go Hang a Salami—I'm a Lasagna Hog* (1991)

Golden Days Puzzlers' Directory Mystic (Randolph C. Lewis), *The Golden Days Puzzlers' Directory* (1886)

Handy-Book William Sheppard Walsh, *The Handy-Book of Literary Curiosities* (1892; 1904)

I Love Me, Vol. I Michael Donner, *I Love Me, Vol. I, S. Wordrow's Palindrome Encyclopedia* (1996)

Language on Vacation Dmitri A. Borgmann, *Language on Vacation: An Olio of Orthographical Oddities* (1965)

Longman Rik J. Edwards, *Longman Anagram Dictionary* (1985)

Making the Alphabet Dance Ross Eckler, *Making the Alphabet Dance; Recreational Wordplay* (1996)

Masquerade *The Masquerade*, six volumes (1797–1806); chapter "Transpositions," edited by George Wilkie

Merry's Puzzles John Newton, *Robert Merry's Second Book of Puzzles* (ca. 1860)

More Joy of Lex Gyles Brandreth, *More Joy of Lex* (1982)

New Anagrammasia Ross Eckler, *The New Anagrammasia; Word Ways* monograph no. 2 (1991); revised edition of Amaranth's (Newton B. Lovejoy) "Anagrammasia"

New Sphinx *The New Sphinx* (1806)

O&C see *Oddities & Curiosities*

Oddities & Curiosities Martin Gardner, *Oddities & Curiosities of Words & Literature* (1961) This is an updated version of Charles Carroll Bombaugh, *Gleanings for the Curious from the Harvest Fields of Literature*, 3rd edition (1890).

OED *The Oxford English Dictionary* (1971) and supplements. All *OED* text references are to the 1971 edition.

Of Anagrams Henry Benjamin Wheatley, *Of Anagrams* (1862)

On Vacation see *Language on Vacation*

Oxford Guide Tony Augarde, *The Oxford Guide to Word Games* (1984)

Palindromes G. R. Clarke, *Palindromes* (1887)

Palindromicon Jeff Grant, *The Palindromicon; Word Ways* monograph no. 3 (1992)

P&A Howard W. Bergerson, *Palindromes & Anagrams* (1973)

Pictured Puzzles & Wordplay Arthur Cyril Pearson, *Pictured Puzzles & Wordplay* (1908)

Portable Curmudgeon Jon Winokur, *The Portable Curmudgeon* (1987)

PP&W see *Pictured Puzzles & Wordplay*

Puzzleana *Puzzleana*, 13th edition (1990); publications in the library of Will Shortz

Puzzledom in a Nutshell Henry E. Juergens and James A. Woolf, *Puzzledom in a Nutshell*, chapter "Names, Noms de Plume & Addresses of Puzzlers" (1877)

Rats Live Joaquin Kuhn and Maura Kuhn, *Rats Live on No Evil Star: The Backwords Puzzle Book* (1981)

Real Puzzles John Q. Boyer, Rufus T. Strohm, and George H. Pryor, *Real Puzzles: Handbook of the Enigmatic Art* (1925)

Remains William Camden, *Remains* (1605)

20th Cent. Book Arthur Cyril Pearson, *The Twentieth-Century Book of Puzzles* (1915)

20th Cent. Standard Arthur Cyril Pearson, *The Twentieth-Century Standard Puzzle Book* (1907)

Periodicals & Popular Puzzle Columns

American Agriculturist *American Agriculturist*; column "New Puzzles to Solve," 1857–1871

American Exchange & Mart *The American Exchange & Mart (& Household Journal)*; Boston and New York; 1886–1887

American Farmer *American Farmer*, Washington, D.C., and Baltimore; column "The Enigma," edited by R. O. Chester (Charles H. Coons), 1894–1897

American N&Q *American Notes & Queries*; Philadelphia journal; edited by William Sheppard Walsh and H. C. Walsh

AP *The Ardmore Puzzler*, Ardmore, Pennsylvania; column "Merion Maze," edited by Remardo (Edwin Smith), 1899–1909

Athenaeum *The Athenaeum*; London; weekly journal

Atlantic Unbound *Atlantic Unbound*, computer on-line *The Atlantic Monthly*; column "Word Games," edited by Emily Cox and Henry Rathvon

Baltimore Item *The Baltimore Item*; newspaper column "Marginalia," edited by Hal Hazard (James R. Price), 1880–1881

Baltimore Sunday News *Baltimore Sunday News*; column "Salmagundi," edited by Maud Lynn (Harry C. Vansant), 1881–1883

B&O *Baltimore & Ohio Magazine*, column "In the Realm of the Riddle," edited by Miss Fitts (Eugene H. Pryor), 1922–1932

Bath Gazette *Bath Gazette*; Bath, England

Central NJ Times *Central New Jersey Times*; Plainfield, New Jersey; column "Guess Work," edited by Eureka (George P. Taggart), 1886–1887

Chambers' Journal, *Chambers' Journal*, London and Edinburgh; "Anagrams, Ancient and Modern"

Chicago Daily Tribune *Chicago Daily Tribune*; column "Puzzler's Corner," edited by Old Man of the C., 1877–1880

Eastern Enigma see *TEE*

Engima see *TE*

Eurekan *The Eurekan*; San Francisco; broadside, 1893–1894, 1902–1904

Evening Telegraph *Daily Evening Telegraph*; Philadelphia; column "Telegraph Twisters," edited by D. C. Ver (George B. King), 1904–1907

Everyman *Everyman*; London weekly magazine; column "Prose & Verse Competitions"

Farmer's Almanac *The Old Farmer's Almanac*; annuals

Farmer's Almanack *The Farmer's Almanack;* Boston; founded 1792; printed earliest American puzzle column, 1802; now called *The Old Farmer's Almanac*

Farmer's Wife *The Farmer's Wife;* St. Paul, Minnesota; column "In Mystic Mood," edited by Kappa Kappa (Clara C. Wouters) and Fred Domino (H. Grady Peery), 1905–1912

F-SP *The Four-Star Puzzler*; New York; 1981–1983

Games *Games*; Ambler, Pennsylvania, and New York

Games & Puzzles *Games & Puzzles*; London, and Luton, England; 1972–1981

GD see *Golden Days*

Gentleman *The Gentleman*; New York; column "Puzzleland," edited by C. Saw (Lewis Truckenbrodt), 1897–1899

Golden Days *Golden Days for Boys & Girls*; Philadelphia weekly; column "Puzzledom," edited by Mystic (Randolph C. Lewis) and others, 1880–1895, and by Arty Fishel (Theodore G. Meyer), 1896–1906

Harper's Young People *Harper's Young People*; New York; column "Puzzles from Young Contributors," edited by Koe (Louis Koelle), 1880–1891

Home Monthly *The Home Monthly*; Pittsburgh, Pennsylvania; column "Quizzisms," edited by The Poser (Henry E. Juergens), 1897–1898

Independent *The Independent*; New York weekly; column "Odd Knots," edited by Erlon R. Chadbourn, 1894–1896

Inter-Ocean *Daily Inter-Ocean, Sunday Inter-Ocean,* or *Weekly Inter-Ocean*; Chicago; column "Complications," edited by Erlon R. Chadbourn, 1881–1914

London Evening Standard *The London Evening Standard*; column edited by Arthur Cyril Pearson, ca. 1900–1905

Macmillan's *Macmillan's Magazine*; article "Anagrams & All Their Kin"

Mensa Bulletin *Mensa Bulletin*; Fort Worth, Texas; official organ of Mensa; column "Wordplay," edited by Bob Kusnetz

MM "Mystic Maze," *Cincinnati Weekly Times*, 1879–1884

Modern Sphinx *The Modern Sphinx*; Santa Clara, California; puzzle journal, first series, 1879

NA *The Newark Advertiser* and *The Newark Daily Advertiser*; Newark, New Jersey; column "The Newark Puzzler," edited by Abel Em (A. Barent Le Massena), 1904–1907, as official organ of the Newark Puzzle Club

N&Q *Notes & Queries*, London

Newark Call *The Newark Call*, a daily, and *The Newark Sunday Call*; Newark, New Jersey; column "Puzzle Calls" and others, 1875–1891; edited by Will A. Mette (William V. Belknap), 1881–1886

Newark Puzzler *The Newark Puzzler*, Newark, New Jersey; edited by Adonis (Herman E. L. Beyer), first series, 1882–1885

New Monthly Magazine *The New Monthly Magazine*, "On Palindromes," 1821

New Statesman *The New Statesman*; London weekly journal; column "Weekend Competition"

NT *The National Tribune*; Washington, D.C.; column "Mystery," edited by Youandi (Charles H. Coons and Eugene J. Hazard), 1891–1897

NY Recorder *New York Recorder*, column "Pastimes," edited by Phil O. Sopher (Oswald C. Drew), 1893

NY Times Magazine *The New York Times Magazine*, column "On Language," edited by William Safire

O'London's *John O'London's Weekly*; London; column "Literary Competitions," edited by Tantalus (William T. Williams), 1928–1945

Oracle *The Oracle;* Newburgh, New York; Newburyport, Pennsylvania; and Pittsburgh; edited by Beech Nut (Brainerd P. Emery), 1896–1899, 1905–1910

Our Boys & Girls *Our Boys & Girls*, also called *Oliver Optic's Magazine;* Boston; column "Headwork," edited by Oliver Optic (William Taylor Adams), 1867–1875

Our Young Folks *Our Young Folks* magazine; Boston; columns "Our Letter Box" and "Round the Evening Lamp," edited by Lucy Larcom, 1865–1873

Owl *The Owl; Wednesday Journal of Politics & Society*; London, 1866 or 1867

Palindromist *The Palindromist;* San Francisco; quarterly edited by Mark Saltveit, 1996–present

Pearson's Weekly *Pearson's Weekly*; London; edited by Arthur Cyril Pearson

Pittsburgh Post *The Pittsburgh Post*; Sunday column "Enigmatic Oddities," edited by Erlon R. Chadbourn, 1900–1910

Puzzletown Oracle *The Puzzletown Oracle*; Newburgh, New York; monthly amateur puzzle broadside, forerunner of *The Oracle* and successor of *Thedom*, all edited by Beech Nut (Brainerd P. Emery), 1896

Saturday Evening Post *Saturday Evening Post*; column "Cerebrations," edited by Wilkins Micawber (E. C. Rideout), 1879–1880

Science Digest Science Digest; New York; column "Puzzles, Paradoxes, Pitfalls," edited by Dr. Crypton (Paul Hoffman), 1983

Scientific American *Scientific American*; column "Mathematical Games," edited by Martin Gardner, 1956–1981

Somerset Messenger *Somerset Messenger*; Somerville, New Jersey; column "Cabala," edited by Calvin (H. C. Vanderveer), 1895–1899

St. Nicholas *St. Nicholas*; New York; monthly juvenile magazine; column "The Riddle Box," edited by Mary Mapes Dodge, ca. 1875

Study *The Study*; Philadelphia; bimonthly amateur magazine and broadside, edited by Anise Lang (Agnes Rosenkrans), 1889–1890

Sunday Standard *The Sunday Standard*; Newark, New Jersey; column "Our Puzzles," edited by Erlon R. Chadbourn, 1894

TE *The Enigma*; official organ of the National Puzzlers' League; column "Penetralia," 1920–present; edited by Arty Ess (Rufus T. Strohm), 1923–1953; currently edited by Xemu (Guy Jacobson); Bridgewater, New Jersey

TEE *The Eastern Enigma*; official organ of the Eastern Puzzler's League, 1883–1910; column "Penetralia," 1900–1902, 1910–1920; magazine retitled in 1920 *The Enigma*, organ of the National Puzzlers' League

Thedom *Thedom*; Newburgh, New York; amateur puzzle broadside, edited by Beech Nut (Brainerd P. Emery), 1889–1895

TS *The Sphinx*; Savannah, Georgia; column "New Puzzles," edited by Tunste (Paul M. Bryan), 1901

Verbatim quarterly magazine, Old Lyme, Connecticut, edited by Lawrence Urdang, 1974–1997

Wall Street Journal *The Wall Street Journal*

Washington Post *The Washington Post*; column "Our Puzzle Department," edited by Carl/ Charles Decker, 1882–1885

Waverley *Waverley Magazine*; Boston; column "Mystic Argosy," edited by Primrose (John Q. Boyer), 1897–1905

WF *Word Fun*; Lockhart, Texas; Mensa SIG newsletter edited by Ken Elrod, 1989–to present; column edited by Kent L. Aldershof

Windsor Magazine *Windsor Magazine*; London; column edited by Arthur Cyril Pearson, ca. 1905

WW *Word Ways: The Journal of Recreational Linguistics*; Morristown, New Jersey; edited by A. Ross Eckler; formerly edited by Dmitri A. Borgmann and Howard W. Bergerson; column "Kickshaws," edited by David Morice and others

WWW *World-Wide Web*, computer site, various "pages": Brian Hall's "Public Domain Palindrome Page," 1995; John Jensen, "Official Palindrome Page," 1995; Neil (Fred) Picciotto's "Gigantic List of Palindromes," Dec. 1, 1995; Jouko I. Valta's "International Palindromes" page, Dec. 1995

YC *The Youth's Companion*; Boston; column "Nuts to Crack," edited by Uncle Tangler (Carlton B. Case) and others, 1871–1929

Organized Puzzlers

The Eastern Puzzlers' League (EPL), established in New York, New York, July 4, 1883, published the magazine *The Eastern Enigma* from Oct. 1883 until 1910 at irregular intervals. In Jan. 1920, the magazine name was changed to *The Enigma* and the organization name to the National Puzzlers' League (NPL).

While other, smaller, puzzlers' organizations exist, the NPL and its predecessor, the EPL, are the most active and are well represented here. The league is the world's oldest puzzlers' association.

Puzzlers & Their Pseudonyms

Pseudonyms are in italics for easy discovery. Some real names are unknown; those in doubt are followed by a question mark. Some locations are unknown, and, of course, cities or towns of puzzlers may change.

A. Barent Le Massena Newark, New Jersey; aka *Abel Em*

Abel Em A. Barent Le Massena; Newark, New Jersey

Ab Struse David Shulman; New York, New York

A. Chem Helen M. (Mrs. Coleman) Miller; Virginia Beach, Virginia

Agnes Rosenkrans Oconomowoc, Wisconsin; aka *Anise Lang*

Ahmed George M. Woodcock; Buffalo, New York

Ai Arthur Schulman; Charlottesville, Virginia

Air Raid H. H. Bailey; London, England

Alan Frank Arlington, Virginia; aka *Alf*

Albert H. Homburg Baltimore, Maryland; aka *Atlas*

Alec Sander E. J. Rodden; Philadelphia, Pennsylvania

Alf Alan Frank; Arlington, Virginia

Al Gebra Robert Hooke; Pittsburgh, Pennsylvania

Alice Lee Newport, Michigan; aka Madda Boutem

A. L. S. Annie Lanman Smith; Urbana, Illinois

Amaranth Newton B. Lovejoy; Pittsburgh, Pennsylvania

Anise Lang Agnes Rosenkrans; Oconomowoc, Wisconsin

Annie Lanman Smith Urbana, Illinois; aka *A. L. S.*

Ann S. Thetics William George Jordan; Philadelphia, Pennsylvania

Anonyme William Grossman; New York, New York

A. Prestin Mellish Providence, Rhode Island; aka *Dreamer*

Arcanus J. E. Reizenstein; Iowa City, Iowa

Archimedes Dr. Harry Langman; Brooklyn, New York

A. R. Graser Philadelphia, Pennsylvania; aka *King Carnival*

Arthur Cyril Pearson (Rev. Arthur Cyril Pearson); London, England

Arthur K. Harris Rumson, New Jersey; aka *Hart King*

Arthur Schulman Charlottesville, Virginia; aka *Ai*

Arty Ess Rufus T. Strohm; Scranton, Pennsylvania

Arty Fishel Theodore G. Meyer; Philadelphia, Pennsylvania
Atlantic Mark Oshin; Portland, Oregon
Atlantis V. E. Beckley; Lima, Ohio
Awl Wrong Patrick J. Flavin; Dorchester, Massachusetts
Balmar Frank T. Koons; Baltimore, Maryland
Barnyard Edward W. Barnard; Fall River, Massachusetts
Beech Nut Brainerd P. Emery; Newburgh, New York
Benjamin C. Pearson location unknown
Betsy Mirarchi Baltimore, Maryland
Blackstone Paul E. Thompson; Allstead, New Hampshire
Bolis George B. Haywood; Rutherford, New Jersey
Brainerd P. Emery Newburgh, New York; aka *Beech Nut*
Brian Hall location unknown
C. A. H. Greene New York, New York
Calvin H. C. Vanderveer; Whitehouse, New Jersey
Camillus real name unknown; Chicago, Illinois
Carlton B. Case Boston, Massachusetts; aka *Uncle Tangler*
Carrol Mayors Roswell, New Mexico; aka *Neophyte*
Carter R. Bennett, Jr. Kilgore, Texas; aka *Plain Text*
Castet G. C. Nichols; Berlin, West Germany
Cephas Peter H. Thomson; Minden, Nebraska
C. F. McCormick Binghamton, New York; aka *Pygmalion*
Charles Decker (Carl); Washington, D.C.
Charles E. Holding Silver Spring, Maryland; aka *Mephisto*
Charles H. Coons Pittsburgh, Pennsylvania; aka *R. O. Chester*
  and *Youandi*
Charles Lutwidge Dodgson England; aka *Lewis Carroll*
Chin Chin real name unknown
Clara C. Wouters Hawley, Minnesota; aka *Kappa Kappa*
Cornel G. Ormsby West Sacramento, California
Correl Kendall Boston, Massachusetts; aka *Sphinx*
Coxy real name unknown; Newark, New Jersey
Crossman, Jr. first name unknown; location unknown
C. Saw Lewis Truckenbrodt (changed in 1916 to Trent); New
  York, New York
C. T. Burroughs Brooklyn, New York; aka *Moonshine*
Damonomad George C. Lamb; Burton, Ohio
Dana Richards Indianapolis, Indiana; aka *George Groth*
Daniel F. Savage Hopkinsville, Kentucky; aka *Delian*
Darryl H. Francis Sutton, England; aka *Lyrrad*
Dauntless Harry P. Leonard; New York, New York

David Ellis Dickerson Tucson, Arizona; aka *Deacon*

David J. Ray San Francisco, California

David L. Silverman West Los Angles, California; aka *Stilicho*

Dave Morice Iowa City, Iowa; aka *Joyce Holland*

David Shulman New York, New York; aka *Ab Struse*

D. C. Ver George B. King; Philadelphia, Pennsylvania

Deacon David Ellis Dickerson; Tucson, Arizona

Delian Daniel F. Savage; Hopkinsville, Kentucky

Dmitri A. Borgmann Oak Park, Illinois; Dayton, Washington; aka *El Uqsor*

Double H Henry Hook; East Rutherford, New Jersey

Douglas Fink Norwalk, Connecticut; aka *Sphinx* and *Non Sequitur*

Dr. Crypton Paul Hoffman, New York, New York

Dreamer A. Prestin Mellish; Providence, Rhode Island

D. Scott Marley Albany, California; aka *Hudu*

E. C. Rideout Philadelphia, Pennsylvania; aka *Wilkins Micawber*

Edgar Allan Poe New York, New York

Edward R. Wolpow Brookline, Massachusetts; aka *Newrow*

Edward Scher location unknown

Edward W. Barnard Fall River, Massachusetts; aka *Barnyard*

Edwin Fitzpatrick Howard W. Bergerson; Sweet Home, Oregon

Edwin Smith Ardmore, Pennsylvania; aka *Remardo*

E. H. Campbell Pittsburgh, Pennsylvania; aka *Neophyte*

E. J. McIlvane Washington, D.C.; aka *Enavlicm*

E. J. Rodden Philadelphia, Pennsylvania; aka *Alec Sander*

Ellen Auriti Oakland, California

Ellsworth Norman E. Nelson; Fort Worth, Texas

El Uqsor Dmitri A. Borgmann; Oak Park, Illinois; Dayton, Washington

Emily Cox and **Henry Rathvon** Hershey, Pennsylvania; aka *Hex*

Emily P. Arulpragasam location unknown

Emmo W. M(elvin). O. Wellman; Lansing, Michigan

Enavlicm E. J. McIlvane; Washington, D.C.

Eric Eric Albert; Auburndale, Massachusetts

Eric Albert Auburndale, Massachusetts; aka *Eric*

Erik Bodin Norfolk, Virginia; aka *Viking*

Erich WR location unknown

Erlon R. Chadbourn Lewiston, Maine

Ernest Ernest W. Ager; Navesink, New Jersey

Ernest W. Ager Navesink, New Jersey; aka *Ernest*

E. S. Crow Capt. William B. Kirk; Lima, Ohio

Ess Ell Irene Fullarton; Silver Lake, New Jersey
Eugene J. Ulrich Enid, Oklahoma; aka *Ulk*
Everett Ewing Norfolk, Virginia; aka *Hi Kerr*
Evergreen Frank G. Mills; Wauwatosa, Wisconsin
E. W. Dutcher Edward William Dutcher; Fulton, Illinois; aka *Towhead*
FaRo (Dr. A.) Ross Eckler; Morristown, New Jersey
F. E. Nash Fort Wayne, Indiana; aka *Hexagony*
Francolin Frank M. Walling; Meadville, Pennsylvania
Frank G. Mills Wauwatosa, Wisconsin; aka *Evergreen*
Frank L. Foss West Mentor, Ohio; aka *Frans Folks*
Frank M. Walling Meadville, Pennsylvania; aka *Francolin*
Frank T. Koons Baltimore, Maryland; aka *Balmar*
Frans Folks Frank L. Foss; West Mentor, Ohio
Fred Domino H. Grady Peery; Corinth, Mississippi
Fred J. Abrahams New York, New York
G. C. Nichols Berlin, West Germany; aka *Castet*
Gemini William R. Hooper; Brooklyn, New York
George B. Haywood Rutherford, New Jersey; aka *Bolis*
George B. King Philadelphia, Pennsylvania; aka *D. C. Ver*
George Chaiyar New York, New York
George Groth Dana Richards; Indianapolis, Indiana
George H. Pryor Baltimore, Maryland; aka *Miss Fitts*
George M. Woodcock Buffalo, New York; aka *Ahmed*
Gertrude Rowe location unknown
G. J. Blundell England
Graham Levi G. De Lee; West Meriden, Connecticut
Graham Reynolds location unknown
G. R. Clarke Glasgow, Scotland
Guy Jacobson Bridgewater, New Jersey; aka *Xemu*
Hal Ober location unknown
Harlan J. Murphy Yazoo City, Mississippi; aka *Spud*
Harry Langman Brooklyn, New York; aka *Archimedes*
Harry Ober Boston, Massachusetts; aka *Hoho*
Harry P. Leonard New York, New York; aka *Dauntless*
Hart King Arthur K. Harris; Rumson, New Jersey
H. C. Vansant Baltimore, Maryland; aka *Maud Lynn* and *Verdant Green*
Helen M. Miller Virginia Beach, Virginia; aka *A. Chem*
Henry Calvin Vanderveer Whitehouse, New Jersey; aka *Calvin*
Henry Campkin England

Henry C. Wiltbank New York, New York; aka *Nypho*

H(enry). E. Juergens Pittsburgh, Pennsylvania; aka *The Poser*

Henry Hook East Rutherford, New Jersey; aka *Double H*

Henry Rathvon and **Emily Cox** Hershey, Pennsylvania; aka *Hex*

Hercules Howard B. McPherrin; Denver, Colorado

Herman E. L. Beyer Newark, New Jersey; aka *Adonis*

Hex Emily Cox and Henry Rathvon; Hershey, Pennsylvania

Hexagony F. E. Nash; Fort Wayne, Indiana

H. Grady Peery Corinth, Mississippi; aka *Fred Domino*

H. H. Bailey London, England; aka *Air Raid*

Hi Kerr Everett Ewing; Norfolk, Virginia

H. J. Wismar Sherman Oaks, California; aka *Pacifico*

Hoho Harry Ober; Boston, Massachusetts

Hoodwink James Lloyd Hood; Bastrop, Texas

Hoosier Theodore A. Funk; Detroit, Michigan

Howard B. McPherrin Denver, Colorado; aka *Hercules*

Howard Richler Côte-Saint-Luc, Quebec; aka *Retrosorter*

Howard W. Bergerson Sweet Home, Oregon; aka *Edwin Fitzpatrick*

Hudu D. Scott Marley; Albany, California

Hugh Hazelrigg location unknown

Ida Poete Waccamaw, South Carolina; aka *Saxon*

Irene Fullarton Silver Lake, New Jersey; aka *Ess Ell*

J. A. Lindon James A. Lindon; Weybridge, England

Jamaica John J. McAlinney; Pittsburgh, Pennsylvania

James C. P. location unknown

James I. Rambo San Francisco, California; aka *Tut*

James Lloyd Hood Bastrop, Texas; aka *Hoodwink*

Jane Prins location unknown

Jason J. J. Bradley; New York, New York

Jed Martinez Margate, Florida; aka *Te-Zir-Man*

Jeff Grant Hastings, New Zealand

Jemand McCulloch B. Wilson; Wilmington, North Carolina

J. E. Reizenstein Iowa City, Iowa; aka *Arcanus*

Jessie McPherrin Denver, Colorado

Jim Beloff Los Angeles, California

J. J. Bradley James Jason Bradley; New York, New York; aka *Jason*

Joaquin Kuhn Fenelon Falls, Ontario

John E. Connett Minneapolis, Minnesota; aka *Rosco X. Ocsor*

John Hesemann location unknown

John Jensen location unknown
John J. McAlinney Pittsburgh, Pennsylvania; aka *Jamaica*
John Leavy location unknown
John Meade location unknown
John M. Meyer Walton, New York; aka *Smith, Tim S.*
John Pool location unknown
John Q. Boyer Baltimore, Maryland; aka *Primrose*
John Taylor England; called the Water Poet, but not a pseudonym
Jon Agee New York, New York
Josefa Heifetz Byrne Mill Valley, California
Jouko I. Valta Oulu, Finland
Judith (Eisenstein) Bagai Portland, Oregon; aka *Sibyl*
Kamel Kathryn Ludlam; St. Petersburg, Florida
Kappa Kappa Clara C. Wouters; Hawley, Minnesota
Kathryn Ludlam St. Petersburg, Florida; aka *Kamel*
Kea Roger Phillips; London, England
Ken Elrod Lockhart, Texas
Kenneth William A. Moore, Jr.; Morton Park, Illinois
K. F. Ross New York, New York
King Carnival A. R. Graser; Philadelphia, Pennsylvania
King Cotton Alfred Snyder; Philadelphia, Pennsylvania
Koe Louis Koelle; New York, New York
Lane Ambler Ove Ofteness; Alameda, California
Larry Loris B. Curtis; Mason, Michigan
L. C. real name unknown
Lee Sallows Nijmegen, Netherlands
Leigh Mercer London, England; aka *Roger G. M'Gregor*
Len Elliott location unknown
Leslie E. Card Urbana, Illinois
Levi G. De Lee West Meriden, Connecticut; aka *Graham*
Lewis Carroll Charles Lutwidge Dodgson; England
Lewis Truckenbrodt (Trent) (Truckenbrodt changed to Trent in
  1916); New York, New York; aka *C. Saw*
Linda Bosson New York, New York; aka *Mona Lisa*
Livedevil William Lutwiniak; Jersey City, New Jersey
Lord Baltimore Simon J. Block; Baltimore, Maryland
Loris B. Curtis Mason, Michigan; aka *Larry*
Louisa H. Sheriden England (d. 1841)
Louis Koelle New York, New York; aka *Koe*
LP Flash real name unknown
Lubin real name unknown; England

Lucy Larcom Boston, Massachusetts
Lycophron Thrace
Lyrrad Darryl H. Francis; Sutton, England
Mabel P. Mabel Poete; Waccamaw, South Carolina
Mabel Poete Waccamaw, South Carolina; aka *Mabel P.*
Madda Boutem Alice Lee; Newport, Michigan
Malcolm Tent Ove Ofteness; Alameda, California
MargB real name unknown
Mark Oshin Portland, Oregon; aka *Atlantic*
Mark Saltveit San Francisco, California
Martin Gardner Hendersonville, North Carolina
Mary C. Snyder Springfield, Illinois; aka *M. C. S.*
Mary J. Hazard née Youngquist; Rochester, New York; aka
   Nightowl
Matilda real name unknown
Matthew K. Franklin location unknown
Maura Kuhn Toronto, Ontario
Maxey Brooke Sweeny, Texas
McCulloch B. Wilson Wilmington, North Carolina; aka *Jemand*
M. C. S. Mary C. Snyder; Springfield, Illinois
Medius real name unknown; Farmington, Connecticut
Melvin O. Wellman Lansing, Michigan; aka *Emmo W.*
Mephisto Charles E. Holding; Silver Spring, Maryland
Merlin Murray R. Pearce; Bismarck, North Dakota
Michael Donner aka *S. Wordrow*
Michael Taub Philadelphia, Pennsylvania
Micky Mackenzie Grand Rapids, Michigan
Mike Griffin location unknown
Mike Morton Waipahu, Hawaii
Minnie Mum Mrs. Paul Smith; Maplewood, New Jersey
Miss L. Booth Cloverdale, Virginia; aka *Palea*
Miss T. Ree Mrs. H. P. Taggert; Plainfield, New Jersey
Molemi Morton Lewis Mitchell; St. Louis, Missouri
Mona Lisa Linda Bosson; New York, New York
Moonshine C. T. Burroughs; Brooklyn, New York
Morton L. Mitchell St. Louis, Missouri; aka *Molemi*
M. O. Wellman Lansing, Michigan; aka *Emmo W.*
Mrs. E. J. Tillman Cambridge, Minnesota; aka *Svensk Grandy-bo*
Mrs. Harris William L. Ougheltree; New York, New York
Mrs. Henry Eagleton Norfolk, Virginia; aka *Su San*
Mrs. H. P. Leonard New York, New York; aka *Seer*

Mrs. H. P. Taggert Plainfield, New Jersey, aka *Miss T. Ree*
Mrs. M. K. Barnes Cape Town, South Africa
Mrs. Paul Smith Maplewood, New Jersey; aka *Minnie Mum*
Mrs. S. F. Bardwell Whitney Crossings, New York; aka *Spica*
Murray R. Pearce Bismarck, North Dakota; aka *Merlin*
M. Victor Goodrich Rock Falls, Illinois; aka *Swamp Angel*
Natalie Heiman location unknown
Neil (Fred) Picciotto location unknown
Neophyte Carrol Mayors; Roswell, New Mexico; 1977 puzzle
Neophyte Edgar H. Campbell; Pittsburgh, Pennsylvania; 1896
   and 1906 puzzles
Newrow Edward R. Wolpow; Brookline, Massachusetts
Newton B. Lovejoy Pittsburgh, Pennsylvania; aka *Amaranth*
Nibbs R. L. Dow; Hartford, Connecticut
Nightowl Mary J. Hazard, née Youngquist; Rochester, New York
N. Jineer Olive W. Dennis; Baltimore, Maryland
Noah R. Deneau Austin, Texas
Noble Holderread Milford, Indiana; aka *Sakr-El-Bahr*
N. O'Body Herman C. Boehme; New York, New York
Non Sequitur Douglas Fink; Norwalk, Connecticut
Norman E. Nelson Fort Worth, Texas; aka *Ellsworth*
Nyas William S. Clarke; Washington, D.C.
O. C. Drew Brooklyn, New York; aka *Phil O. Sopher*
Olive W. Dennis Baltimore, Maryland; aka *N. Jineer*
O. M. Ove Ofteness; Alameda, California
O. N. E. One John Nesbit; New York, New York
Ove Ofteness Alameda, California; aka *Lane Ambler*, *Malcolm
   Tent*, *O.M.*, *O. V. Michaelsen*, and *Rom Dos*
O. V. Michaelsen Ove Ofteness; Alameda, California
Pacifico H. J. Wismar; Sherman Oaks, California
Palea Miss L. Booth; Cloverdale, Virginia
Patrick J. Flavin Dorchester, Massachusetts; aka *Awl Wrong*
Patrick Robbins location unknown
Paul E. Thompson Cleveland Heights, Ohio; aka *Blackstone*
Paul Hoffman New York, New York; aka *Dr. Crypton*
Peter Hilton Binghamton, New York
Peter H. Thomson Minden, Nebraska; aka *Cephas*
Peter L. Stein San Francisco, California
Peter Newby Chesterfield, England; aka *Walter Fretlaw*
Peter N. Horne Seattle, Washington
Philip Morse location unknown

PikMee John Raguso; location unknown
Plain Text Carter R. Bennett, Jr.; Kilgore, Texas
Primrose John Q. Boyer; Baltimore, Maryland
Pygmalion C. F. McCormick; Binghamton, New York
Pythagoras Greece
Q William Lawrence; Mount Vernon, New York
R real name unknown
R. Are real name unknown
Remardo Edwin Smith; Ardmore, Pennsylvania
Retrosorter Howard Richler; Côte-Saint-Luc, Quebec
R. G. Robert Gillespie?; Brooklyn, New York
Richard Lederer San Diego, California
Rizpah real name unknown; Baltimore, Maryland
R. L. Dow Hartford, Connecticut; aka *Nibbs*
Robert G. Evans Holland, Michigan; aka *Wrong Font*
Robert Gillespie Brooklyn, New York; aka *R. G.?*
Robert Hooke Pittsburgh, Pennsylvania; aka *Al Gebra*
Robert P. King Erie, Pennsylvania; aka *Sans Souci*
Robert S. Dow Newark, New Jersey
Robert Siegel location unknown
Robert Ustrich Los Angeles, California; aka *Sol, Jr.*
R. O. Chester Charles H. Coons; Pittsburgh, Pennsylvania
Roger G. M'Gregor Leigh Mercer; London, England
Roger Phillips London, England; aka *Kea*
Rom Dos Ove Ofteness; Alameda, California
Ron Howes location unknown
Rosalie Moscovitch Côte-Saint-Luc, Quebec; aka *Wabbit*
Rosco X. Ocsor John E. Connett; Minneapolis, Minnesota
Ross Eckler Morristown, New Jersey; aka *FaRo*
Rufus T. Strohm Scranton, Pennsylvania; aka *Arty Ess* and *R.T.S.*
Ruth Ruth Germann; Newark, New Jersey
Ruth Germann Newark, New Jersey; aka *Ruth*
Ruth Herbert Palo Alto, California; aka *Ruthless*
Ruthless Ruth Herbert; Palo Alto, California
Ruthven Edwin R. Briggs; West Bethel, Maine
Sakr-El-Bahr Noble Holderread; Milford, Indiana
Sally Sally Picciotto; New Haven, Connecticut
Sally Picciotto New Haven, Connecticut; aka *Alice* and *Sally*
Sam Weller Torry Kirk; Lima, Ohio
Sans Souci Robert P. King; Erie, Pennsylvania
Saxon Ida Poete; Waccamaw, South Carolina

Seer Mrs. H. P. Leonard; New York, New York
Sibyl Judith E. Bagai; Portland, Oregon
Simon J. Block Baltimore, Maryland; aka *Lord Baltimore*
Skeeziks William L. Ougheltree; New York, New York
S. L. B. real name unknown
Smith, Tim S. John M. Meyer; Walton, New York
Sol, Jr. Robert Ustrich; Los Angeles, California
Sotades Maroneia, Crete, Greece
Sphinx Correl Kendall; Boston, Massachusetts; late 1800s
Sphinx Douglas Fink; Norwalk, Connecticut; 1980s–1990s
Spica Mrs. S. F. Bardwell; Whitney Crossings, New York
Spud Harlan J. Murphy; Yazoo City, Mississippi
Stephan R. Marlow location unknown
Stephen J. Chism Fayetteville, Arkansas
Stephen (Joshua) Sondheim New York, New York
Stilicho David L. Silverman; West Los Angeles, California
Stocles Thomas F. Wood; St. Louis, Missouri
Su San Mrs. Henry Eagleton; Norfolk, Virginia
Susan C. Ridgeway location unknown
Susan Leslie location unknown
Susan Thorpe Buckinghamshire, England
Svensk Grandy-bo Mrs. E. J. Tillman; Cambridge, Minnesota
Swamp **Angel** M. Victor Goodrich; Rock Falls, Illinois
S. Wordrow Michael Donner
Tantalus William T. Williams; London, England
Te-Zir-Man Jed Martinez; Margate, Florida
T. H. Rev. Theodore Hoagland; Moscow, Idaho
The Duke real name unknown
Theodore A. Funk Detroit, Michigan; aka *Hoosier*
Theodore G. Meyer Philadelphia, Pennsylvania; aka *Arty Fishel*
The Poser H. E. Juergens; Pittsburgh, Pennsylvania
Thomas F. Wood St. Louis, Missouri; aka *Stocles*
Timothy J. Wheeler Shelbyville, Indiana; aka *Tweaser*
Tom Allen Iowa City, Iowa; aka *Talon*
Tom Deneau Austin, Texas
Tom Nobel location unknown
Tom Pulliam Somerset, New Jersey
Torry Kirk Lima, Ohio; aka *Traddles* and *Sam Weller*
Towhead Edward W. Dutcher; Fulton, Illinois
T. P. O'Brien location unknown
Traddles Torry Kirk; Lima, Ohio

Tunste Paul M. Bryan; Washington, D.C.

Tut James I(rwin) Rambo; San Francisco, California

Tweaser Timothy J. Wheeler; Shelbyville, Indiana

Ulk Eugene J. Ulrich; Grand Chain, Illinois

V. E. Beckley Lima, Ohio; aka *Atlantis*

Verdant Green Harry C. Vansant; Baltimore, Maryland

Viking Erik Bodin; Norfolk, Virginia

Virginia Dare Virginia D. Jackson; Pennsylvania

Wabbit Rosalie Moscovitch; Côte-Saint-Luc, Quebec

Walter Fretlaw Peter Newby; Chesterfield, England

Wede Willard R. Espy; New York, New York

Wilkins Micawber E. C. Rideout; Philadelphia, Pennsylvania

Will A. Mette William V. Belknap; Newark, New Jersey

Willard R. Espy New York, New York; aka *Wede*

William A. Moore, Jr. Morton Park, Illinois; aka *Kenneth*

William B. Kirk Lima, Ohio; aka *E. S. Crow*

William George Jordon Philadelphia, Pennsylvania; aka *Ann S. Thetics*

William Grossman New York, New York; aka *Anonyme*

William Lawrence Mount Vernon, New York; aka *Q*

William L. Ougheltree New York, New York; aka *Alliteraricus, A. Street Walker, Javelin, Mr. E., Mrs. Harris, O. W. L.,* and possibly *P. Uns*

William L. Sacrey Philadelphia, Pennsylvania; aka Yercas

William Lutwiniak Jersey City, New Jersey; aka *Livedevil*

William Oldys England

William R. Hooper Brooklyn, New York; aka *Gemini*

William S. Clarke Washington, D.C.; aka *Nyas*

William T. Williams London, England; aka *Tantalus*

William V. Belknap William V. Belknap; Newark, New Jersey; aka *Will A. Mette* and *Guillielmus Rex*

William W. Delaney New York, New York; aka *Willie Wildwave*

Willie Wildwave William W. Delaney; New York, New York

Will Shortz Pleasantville, New York; aka *Willz*

Willy Wisp W. G. Scribner?; Lincoln, Nebraska?

Willz Will Shortz; Pleasantville, New York

Winfred S. Emmons Waco, Texas

Wrong Font Robert G. Evans; Holland, Michigan

W. Williams Haverfordwest, Wales

Xemu Guy Jacobson; Bridgewater, New Jersey

Yercas Dr. William L. Sacrey; Philadelphia, Pennsylvania

Acknowledgments

I am especially indebted to the National Puzzlers' League, in which I used the pseudonym Rom Dos; Sheila Anne Barry; my editor, Jeanette Green, for her outstanding work; Howard W. Bergerson, former editor of *Word Ways: The Journal of Recreational Linguistics*, for permission to reprint material from his book *Palindromes & Anagrams* (1973); and Dmitri A. Borgmann, the father of modern "logology" (recreational linguistics), founding editor of *Word Ways*, and author of *Curious Crosswords* (1970), *Beyond Language: Adventures in Word & Thought* (1967), and *Language on Vacation: An Olio of Orthographical Oddities* (1965).

Thanks to my wife, Lois Marin Fischer, for proofreading, suggestions, and technical assistance; the late author Willard R. Espy, to whom I am deeply grateful for planting the seed and for permission to reprint material from his books; puzzlemeister Will Shortz for his invaluable resources, exceptional consideration, and support; Dr. A. Ross Eckler, author of *Making the Alphabet Dance* (1996) and former editor of *The Enigma*, for kindly helping with puzzle sources and dates and for his generous permission to reprint material from *Word Ways*; David Morice, illustrator, editor of "Kickshaws" in *Word Ways* and author of *The Dictionary of Wordplay* (2001); Ken Elrod for permission to reprint quotes from his Mensa SIG newsletter, *Word Fun*; Emily Cox and Henry Rathvon for permission to reprint palindromes from their "Word Games" column in *Atlantic Unbound* (*The Atlantic Monthly* online); Tony Augarde for supplying me with the sources of some of the anagrams quoted in his book *The Oxford Guide to Word Games* (1984); John E. Connett for permission to include his palindromes; Wilder Bentley; Herbert Pfeiffer; Mark Saltveit; Jouko Valta; Dan Tilque for his contributions, corrections and suggestions; Kim Walker-Daniels, former editor of the *Mensa International Journal*; to authors Paul Dickson for thoughtful suggestions, and to Martin Gardner for his key role in making this book a reality.

Quotes from *The Enigma* are reprinted by permission from the National Puzzlers' League.

A fan of the rock group The Doors called my attention to the fact that reshuffling the letters in the words "Mr. Mojo risin'" from the song "L. A. Woman" reveals the name JIM MORRI-SON. While browsing through dictionaries I found rhymes for *orange, silver,* and *purple.* Discoveries like these piqued my interest in word curiosities.

In my research, I perused books dating from the seventeenth century to the present and more than forty puzzle columns in periodicals published in the United States and the United Kingdom since 1866, including privately issued puzzle journals, broadsides, and newsletters.

Wordplay and puzzles have been among my favorite pastimes as long as I can remember, but I must give credit (or blame) to the late author Willard R. Espy for being a major source of my early inspiration. Through his books I discovered the National Puzzlers' League, *Word Ways* magazine, works of Dmitri A. Borgmann, and those of other wordsmiths.

—*O. V. MICHAELSEN*

E-mail: ovmichaelsen@hotmail.com

Web site: http://home.pacbell.net/romdos/index.html

Endnotes

Chapter 3

People
This list of unusual names was collected from many sources. Col. Clarence Clapsaddle, Katz Meow, I. C. Shivers, and Justin Tune were in John Train's *Remarkable Names of Real People* (1977). Genghis Cohen appears in *Even More Remarkable Names* (1979), Groaner Digger in *Most Remarkable Names* (1985), and Judge Law and Judge Judge in Gyles Brandeth's *The Joy of Lex* (1980). Mark Johnson, *WF*, Feb. 1992, discovered Dr. Cheek and Justin Brown, and *WF*, Aug. 1994, the dangerous-sounding Dr. Hatchet.

Ludicrous Acronyms
Sources for these lists of ludicrous acronyms and other peculiar acronyms include Jennifer Mossman's *The Acronyms, Initialisms & Abbreviations Dictionary* (1996), Ralph De Sola's *The Abbreviations Dictionary* (1986), and Paul Hellweg's *The Insomniac's Dictionary* (1986).

Chapter 10

Pseudo-Autonyms
Word Ways collectors have discovered some of these. David Silverman found *catwalk, lowlands, maternity dress,* and *nighthawk* (Feb. 1970); Murray Pearce, *hereafter* and *undergo* (Aug. 1970); and Leslie Card, *hotheads* (Aug. 1970).

Chapter 12

By Definition

Anagrams, Transposals, & Mutations

1. Rik Edwards, *Longman* (1985).
2. Alfred H. Smith, *St. Nicholas*, July 1875.
3. Rik Edwards, *Longman* (1985).
4. O. V. Michaelsen, *WF*, Feb. 1991.

Avoiding Contrived Bases

1. Anglo Saxon, *Inter-Ocean*, Apr. 22, 1902.
2. Ellsworth, *TE*, Jan. 1925.

Headlines & Missing Articles

1. Remardo, *TEE*, Mar. 1915.
2. Yercas, *TE*, Mar. 1933.
3. T. H., *Inter-Ocean*, May 2, 1899.
4. Camillus, *GD*, May 5, 1883.
5. Alf, *TE*, Sept. 1992.
6. Viking, *TE*, Mar. 1934.

Articles at Large

1. Ellsworth, *TE*, Oct. 1933.
2. Kenneth, *Waverley*, Feb. 25, 1899.
3. Viking, *TE*, Feb. 1965.
4. Viking, *TE*, Oct. 1931.

Interjections

1. D. C. Ver, *GD*, Oct. 15, 1898.
2. Enavlicm, *B&O*, Nov. 1931.
3. Ulk, *TE*, Feb. 1993.
4. Wabbit, *TE*, Dec. 1990.

The "I's" Have It

1. Fred Domino, *TE*, June 1951.
2. Tweaser, *TE*, Aug. 1988.
3. S. L. B., *YC*, May 18, 1871.
4. Neophyte, *TE*, May 1977.
5. (a) Alec Sander, *TEE*, June 1919;
   (b) Barnyard, *TEE*, July 1917.
6. Jemand, *TE*, Dec. 1915.
7. Viking, *TE*, Nov. 1933.
8. Minnie Mum, *TE*, July 1925.

Fifty Choice Anagrams
To find full book and periodical titles, look in Key to Abbreviations (p. 172), and to discover a puzzler's identity, check Puzzlers & Their Pseudonyms (p. 180).

1. Ab Struse, *F-SP*, Apr. 1982.
2. Awl Wrong, *TE*, Dec. 1939.
3. Lord Baltimore, *NT*, Feb. 6, 1896.
4. Ess Ell, *NA*, June 2, 1906.
5. Mabel P., *Pittsburgh Post*, Apr. 1, 1900.
6. Amaranth, *TEE*, Feb. 1916.
7. D. C. Ver, *TEE*, June 1919.
8. Su San, *TE*, Feb. 1948.
9. Air Raid, *TE*, Apr. 1920.
10. Rizpah, *Waverley*, Nov. 19, 1898.
11. M. C. S., *Sunday Standard*, Sept. 30, 1894.
12. Enavlicm, *NA*, Jan. 12, 1907.
13. Stephan R. Marlow, *F-SP*, Oct. 1981.
14. Anonyme, *Puzzletown Oracle*, Jan. 15, 1896.
15. Damonomad, *TE*, Mar. 1934.
16. *The New York Times*, 1997.
17. Awl Wrong, *TE*, July 1941.
18. Spud, *TE*, Dec. 1922.
19. Viking, *TE*, July 1931.
20. Sam Weller, *GD*, July 2, 1881.
21. Delian, *TS*, May 1901.
22. O.N.E. One, *NA*, Apr. 20, 1905.

23. D. C. Ver, *GD*, Dec. 4, 1897.
24. *Traddles*, 1880s.
25. Double H, *TE*, Nov. 1983.
26. Kea, *TE*, Oct. 1994.
27. M. C. S., *Inter-Ocean*, Oct. 8, 1901.
28. The Duke, *TEE*, June 1913.
29. Towhead, *TE*, Jan. 1922.
30. Mike Morton, 1995.
31. D. C. Ver, *GD*, July 14, 1897.
32. Atlantic, *TE*, Apr. 1988.
33. Rev. Arthur Pearson, *20th Cent. Book* (1915).
34. Arty Fishel, *Study*, Oct. 22, 1886.
35. N. Jineer, *TE*, May 1925.
36. Q, *TE*, Jan. 1927.
37. Ess Ell, *Inter-Ocean*, Sept. 4, 1908.
38. Viking, *TE*, Feb. 1932.
39. Anon., *P&A* (1973).
40. Josefa Heifetz Byrne, *WW*, May 1970.
41. Awl Wrong, *TE*, July 1940.
42. Arty Ess, *Inter-Ocean*, June 19, 1908.
43. Francolin, *TEE*, Sept. 1915.
44. Atlantis, *TEE*, Feb. 1911.
45. Sakr-el-bahr, *TE*, Apr. 1934.
46. D. C. Ver, *NA*, Aug. 4, 1906.
47. A. Chem, *TE*, Apr. 1930.
48. Darryl Francis, *WW*, Nov. 1968.
49. Skeeziks, *Thedom*, Nov. 10, 1890.
50. Virginia Dare, *TE*, Feb. 1922.

Honorable-Mention Anagrams

1. Nightowl, *TE*, May 1988.
2. Viking, *P&A* (1973).
3. Al Gebra, *TE*, Oct. 1963.
4. Viking, *TE*, Dec. 1933.
5. Molemi, *Oracle*, Jan. 1907.
6. Jessie McPherrin, *TE*, Feb. 1951.
7. Primrose, *Somerset Messenger*, May 18, 1898.
8. N. Jineer, *TE*, Dec. 1923.
9. Molemi, "Anagrammasia" (1926).

10. Awl Wrong, *TE*, July 1940.
11. Fred Domino, *TE*, Aug. 1953.
12. George Groth, *TE*, Aug. 1982.
13. Molemi, *Inter-Ocean*, Jan. 19, 1912.
14. Mona Lisa, *TE*, Feb. 1978.
15. Enavlicm, *TEE*, Nov. 1917.
16. Dreamer, *TE*, Feb. 1926.
17. Pacifico, *TE*, July 1956.
18. Spica, *TEE*, 1917.
19. Awl Wrong, *TE*, Feb. 1944.
20. Merlin, *TE*, Dec. 1971.
21. Kenneth, *Gentleman*, May 1899.
22. Atlantic, *TE*, June 1991.
23. Hudu, *TE*, Jan. 1987.
24. Awl Wrong, *TE*, Dec. 1943.
25. Gemini, *TE*, July 1924.
26. Balmar, *AP*, May 26, 1900.
27. Archimedes, *TE*, Sept. 1938.
28. Viking, *TE*, June 1972.
29. Moonshine, *TE*, Apr. 1927.
30. Hexagony, *Inter-Ocean*, June 12, 1908.
31. Nibbs, *TEE*, Dec. 1898.
32. Wrong Font, *TE*, Feb. 1938.
33. Talon, *TE*, Mar. 1991.
34. Awl Wrong, *TE*, May 1948.
35. Neophyte, *Sunday Standard*, Apr. 12, 1896.
36. Len Elliott, *F-SP*, Aug. 1983.
37. Viking, *TE*, Apr. 1937.
38. Viking, *TE*, Sept. 1964.
39. Viking, *TE*, Oct. 1972.
40. Hercules, *TE*, July 1924.
41. Atlantic, *TE*, Dec. 1982.
42. Tony Augarde, *Oxford Guide* (1984).
43. R. Are, *AP*, Mar. 15, 1907.
44. Viking, *TE*, May 1968.
45. Tut, *TE*, May 1975.
46. Livedevil, *TE*, ca. 1938–1941 (uncertain).
47. Hoodwink, *TE*, Feb. 1955.
48. Hercules, *TE*.
49. Jamaica, *NA*, Aug. 19, 1905.
50. Nypho, *TE*, June 1949.

Less Perfect Anagrams

1. R. O. Chester, *Evening Telegraph*, 1905.
2. E. S. Crow, *TE*, Mar. 1927.
3. Viking, *TE*, May 1931.
4. Arcanus, *NT*, Feb. 17, 1896.
5. Sphinx, *TE*, Nov. 1985.
6. Dmitri Borgmann, *On Vacation* (1965).
7. Tweaser, *TE*, April 1991.
8. Ab Struse, *TE*, July 1984.

One-Word Anagrams

1. Ruth, *St. Nicholas*, Sept. 1876.
2. Kenneth, *Inter-Ocean*, Jan. 31, 1899.
3. King Carnival, *Evening Telegraph*, 1905.
4. *TE*, June 1925.
5. Cephas, *Independent*, Jan. 16, 1896.
7. T. L., *Farmer's Almanack*, 1815.
8. Ellsworth, *TE*, May 1925.
9. Neophyte, *NA*, Aug. 4, 1906.
10. *Inter-Ocean*, Sept. 13, 1896.
11. Francolin, *TE*, Jan. 1915.
13. Rev. Arthur Pearson, *20th Cent. Standard* (1907).
14. Hoho, *TE*, Mar. 1943.
15. Nyas, *NT*, Apr. 11, 1893.
16. Jason, *AP*, Sept. 15, 1902.
17. Anonyme, *TEE*, Dec. 1913.
18. Miss T. Ree, *Central NJ Times*, May 1887.
20. Viking, *TE*, Sept. 1931.
21. Koe, *Harper's Young People*, July 11, 1882.
22. *New Sphinx* (1806).
23. R., *St. Nicholas*, May 1875.
24. Ruth, *St. Nicholas*, Sept. 1876.
25. Beech Nut, *Oracle*, May 1898.

Transposed Couplets, or Pairagrams

1. Viking, *TE*, Feb. 1972.
2. Sol, Jr., *TE*, May 1954.

5. L. M. N. Terry, *AP*, Dec. 1, 1900.
7. Dauntless, *NA*, Jan. 27, 1906.
8. Medius, *Pittsburgh Post*, Mar. 16, 1902.
9. Nyas, *NT*, Nov. 29, 1894.
11. Molemi, *B&O*, Apr. 1928.
12. N. O'Body, *TE*, Apr. 1931.
13. *O'London's*, Oct. 27, 1934.
14. R., *St. Nicholas*, May 1875.
15. Primrose, *Somerset Messenger*, Sept. 23, 1896.
17. Miss H. Selway, *O'London's*, Nov. 30, 1929.
18. Seer, *NA*, June 11, 1904.
20. Swamp Angel, *Inter-Ocean*, Mar. 17, 1895.

Antigrams—Antonymous Anagrams

1. Arcanus, *TEE*, Dec. 1898.
2. Pygmalion, *GD*, Oct. 2, 1886.
3. Sally, *TE*, Oct. 1989.
4. Castet, *TE*, July 1952.
5. Hi Kerr, *TE*, June 1927.
6. D. C. Ver, *NA*, Sept. 8, 1906.
7. Rom Dos, *TE*, July 1992.
8. Viking, *TE*, Oct. 1964.
9. Gemini, *TE*, Oct. 1925.
10. Atlantic, *TE*, Jan. 1993.
11. Hoho, *TE*, Oct. 1960.
12. *Longman* (1985).
13. Hercules, *TE*, Feb. 1928.
14. Te-Zir-Man, *TE*, Jan. 1990.
15. Sphinx, *TE*, June 1986.
16. Non Sequitur, *TE*, Nov. 1992.
17. A. Chem, *TE*, July 1967.
18. Louisa H. Sheridan, ca. 1831–1835; *N&Q*, Oct. 12, 1861.
19. Larry, *TE*, Feb. 1927.
20. Hoodwink, *TE*, Sept. 1948.

Ambigram

1. Te-Zir-Man, *TE*, Feb. 1993.
2. Rom Dos, *WW*, Nov. 2004.

Chapter 13

Anagram Musings

1. Puzzlers responsible for these transformations are Rik Edwards, *Longman* (1985), for Bengali; Rev. Arthur Pearson, *Pictured Puzzles & Wordplay* (1908), for wild boars and (in)sanitary; and Chin-Chin, *Washington Post*, Dec. 9, 1883, for melon.

Cheaters' Anagrams

1. Rik Edwards, *Longman* (1985).
2. Rik Edwards, *Longman* (1985).
3. Deacon, *TE*, Nov. 1990.
4. Rev. Arthur Pearson, *20th Cent. Standard* (1907).
5. O.M., Jan. 2005.

Anagrammatic Cross-References

1. Arty Fishel, *GD*, Mar. 5, 1887.
2. *American Agriculturist*, May 1861.
3. David Morice, *WW*, Feb. 1995.
4. David Morice, *WW*, Feb. 1995.

Hurry to the Rear

1. Hoho, *TE*, Dec. 1941.
2. Dave Morice, *WW*, Nov. 2001

Saint, Santa, Satan

1. Madda Boutem, *TE*, Jan. 1940.
2. Sphinx, *TE*, Feb. 1985.

Anagram Puzzles

1. Arcanus, *TE*, Sept. 1935.
2. Hoho, *TE*, Aug. 1946.
3. Molemi, *TE*, Nov. 1945.
4. Ai, *TE*, Feb. 1994.
5. Amaranth, *Inter-Ocean*, Jan. 13, 1911.
6. O. V. Michaelsen, *TE*, Sept. 1990.
7. Te-Zir-Man, *TE*, Oct. 1989.
8. Atlantic, *TE*, May 1982.
9. Francolin, *TE*, May 1915.
10. Te-Zir-Man, *TE*, May 1987.
11. Ulk, *TE*, Apr. 1986.
12. Ruthless, *TE*, Apr. 1989.
13. Ab Struse, *TE*, Mar. 1988.
14. Kamel, *TE*, Jan. 1982.
15. Atlantic, *TE*, Jan. 1982.
16. Barnyard, *TE*, Oct. 1917.
17. Stocles, *TE*, Mar. 1920.
18. Merlin, *TE*, Oct. 1971.
19. Rom Dos, *TE*, Nov. 1990.
20. Ab Struse, *TE*, Mar. 1980.

Chapter 14

A Palindrome Collection
Letter-Unit Palindromes

First Words

1. (a, b) Michael Donner, *I Love Me, vol. I* (1996).
2. (a) without parentheses, Henry Wheatley, *Of Anagrams* (1862); brackets, Leigh Mercer, *N&Q*, Jan. 10, 1948; parentheses, John Connett, *WW*, May 1996; (b) Henry Wheatley, *Of Anagrams* (1862).
3. Howard Bergerson, *P&A* (1973).
4. Tut, *TE*, Mar. 1974.
5. Atlantis, *AP*, Dec. 1, 1907.

6. (a, b) Rev. Arthur Pearson, *20th Cent. Standard* (1907).

7. (a) Joaquin and Maura Kuhn, *Rats Live* (1981); (b) Ruthven, *Ballou's Monthly*, May 1873.

All at Sea

8. (a) Leigh Mercer, *N&Q*, Feb. 1953; (b) Howard Bergerson, *P&A* (1973).

9. (a, b) Dmitri Borgmann in Martin Gardner, *O&C* (1961); (c) Joaquin and Maura Kuhn, *Rats Live* (1981).

10. (a) M. C. S., *Inter-Ocean*, July 26, 1896; (b) Leigh Mercer, *N&Q*, Feb. 1952.

11. Jon Agee, *Go Hang* (1991).

12. Joaquin and Maura Kuhn, *Rats Live* (1981).

13. J. A. Lindon in Howard Bergerson, *P&A* (1973).

Right, But No Cigar

14. (a) J. A. Lindon in Howard Bergerson, *P&A* (1973); (b) Smith, Tim S., *TE*, Aug. 1975; (c) Smith, Tim S., Oct. 1967.

Drinks All Around

15. Leigh Mercer, N&Q, Nov. 2, 1946.

16. Atlantis, *AP*, Dec. 1, 1907.

18. (a) Howard Bergerson, *P&A* (1973); (b) anonymous; (c) Leigh Mercer, *N&Q*, Nov. 2, 1946.

19. Jon Agee, *Dynamos* (1994).

20. Henry Campkin, *N&Q*, Mar. 8, 1873.

21. J. A. Lindon in Howard Bergerson, *P&A* (1973).

22. *O'London's*, Aug. 31, 1929.

23. (a) Tut, *TE*, Sept. 1974; (b) Graham Reynolds in Howard Bergerson, *P&A* (1973).

24. J. A. Lindon in Howard Bergerson, *P&A* (1973).

25. (a) Michael Taub, *Atlantic Unbound*, Aug. 30, 1996; (b) Dmitri Borgmann, *On Vacation* (1965).

26. Joaquin and Maura Kuhn, *Rats Live* (1981).

Sporting Chances

27. J. A. Lindon in Howard Bergerson, *P&A* (1973).
28. Erich, W. R., *Atlantic Unbound*, Aug. 30. 1996.
29. (a) Joaquin and Maura Kuhn, *Rats Live* (1981); (b) Howard Richler, *WW*, Nov. 1991; (c) LP Flash, *Atlantic Unbound*, Aug. 30, 1996.
30. Atlantis, *GD*, June 7, 1905.
31. (a) Atlantis, *AP*, Dec. 1, 1907; (b) Cornel G. Ormsby; (c) Atlantis, *AP*, Dec. 1, 1907.

Little Wars

32. (a) Howard Bergerson, *P&A* (1973); (b) Martin Gardner, *O&C* (1961).
33. Jouko I. Valta, "International Palindromes" page, *WWW*, Dec. 1995.
34. Ron Howes, *Atlantic Unbound*, Aug. 30, 1996.
35. Howard Richler, *WW*, Feb. 1991.
36. Joaquin and Maura Kuhn, *Rats Live* (1981).
37. George Chaiyar, *NY World*, Dec. 11, 1921.
38. Charles Bombaugh, *Gleanings* (1867).
39. Evergreen, *TE*, June 1956.
40. Tut, *TE*, June 1977.
41. Jon Agee, *Go Hang* (1991).
42. Neil (Fred) Picciotto's "Gigantic List of Palindromes," *WWW*, Dec. 1, 1995.
43. (a) Leigh Mercer, *N&Q*, Nov. 13, 1948; (b) J. A. Lindon's poem title in Howard Bergerson, *P&A* (1973); (c) Rev. Arthur Pearson, *PP&W* (1908); (d) G. R. Clarke, *Palindromes* (1887).
44. Dmitri Borgmann, *On Vacation* (1965).

Food, Glorious Food

45. (a) Howard Richler, *WW*, May 1991; (b) Enavlicm, *TEE*, June 1912; (c) Leigh Mercer, *N&Q*, Nov. 2, 1946; (d) T. P. O'Brien, *London Times*, July 18, 1973; (e) anonymous; (f) Jon Agee, *Dynamos* (1994); (g) *TE*, 1942; Henry Campkin, *N&Q*, Mar. 8, 1873; (h) John Connett, Feb. 1996; (i) O. V. Michaelsen; (j) Howard Richler, *WW*, Nov. 1995

46. (a) Joaquin and Maura Kuhn, *Rats Live* (1981); (b) J. A. Lindon in Howard Bergerson, *P&A* (1973); (c) Joaquin and Maura Kuhn, *Rats Live* (1981); (d) Peter Hilton, 1943; (e) John Connett, May 1996; (f) Coxy, *NA*, Aug. 13, 1904; R. C. O'Brien, *New York World*, Nov. 20, 1921; "not a ton" in G. R. Clarke, *Palindromes* (1887); (g) Jon Agee, *Dynamos* (1994); (h) R, *St. Nicholas*, May 1875; parentheses anonymous; (i) Mabel P., *Pittsburgh Post*, Aug. 5, 1900; (j) John Pool, *Daffodil* (1982); (k) David Woodside, *WW*, Aug. 1996; (l) anonymous.

Wine, Women, & Song

47. Howard Bergerson, *P&A* (1973).
48. (a) *American N&Q*, Jan. 5, 1889; (b) Gertrude Rowe, *Everyman*, Nov. 28, 1929; (c) Leigh Mercer, *N&Q*, Nov. 2, 1946.
49. Dmitri Borgmann, *On Vacation* (1965).
50. (a) J. A. Lindon in Martin Gardner, *Scientific American*, Sept. 1964; (b) anonymous.
51. Dmitri Borgmann, *On Vacation* (1965).
52. Howard Bergerson, *P&A* (1973).
53. (a) R. G., *St. Nicholas*, Feb. 1875; (b) parentheses in G. R. Clarke, *Palindromes* (1887); (c) Leigh Mercer in Howard Bergerson, *P&A* (1973).
54. (a) Howard Richler, *WW*, May 1992; (b) Rev. Arthur Pearson, *20th Cent. Standard* (1907); (c) anonymous; (d) L. C., *O'London's*, Aug. 31, 1929; (e) Jon Agee, *Go Hang* (1991); (f) J. A. Lindon in Howard Bergerson, *P&A* (1973); (g) Ron Howes, *Atlantic Unbound*, Aug. 30, 1996; (h) Howard Bergerson, *P&A* (1973); (i) Michael Helsem, *WW*, May 1991.
55. Tut, *TE*, Apr. 1972.
56. Joaquin and Maura Kuhn, *Rats Live* (1981).
57. Howard Richler, *WW*, May 1993.
58. Tom Nobel, *WW*, May 1995.
59. John Connett, Mar. 1996.
60. Howard Bergerson, *P&A* (1973).
61. Leigh Mercer, *N&Q*, Oct. 16, 1948.

62. Stephen Chism, *From A to Zotamorf* (1992).

63. W. Williams, *Everyman*, Nov. 28, 1929.

64. Dmitri Borgmann, *On Vacation* (1965).

65. John Connett, July 1996.

66. John Pool, *Daffodil* (1982).

67. J. A. Lindon, *WW*, Nov. 1971.

68. (a) Howard Richler, *WW*, Nov. 1991; (b) Michael Gartner, *St. Louis Post-Dispatch*, 1972, in Willard Espy, *An Almanac* (1975); parentheses by anonymous.

69. Charles Bombaugh, *Gleanings* (1890); also Dmitri Borgmann in Martin Gardner, *O&C* (1961); parentheses by anonymous.

70. Graham, *Washington Post*, Sept. 21, 1884.

71. (a) J. A. Lindon, *P&A* (1973); (b) John Connett, Feb. 1996; (c, f–k) Joaquin and Maura Kuhn, *Rats Live* (1981); (d) Dona Smith, *Wo, Nemo! Toss a Lasso to Me, NOW!* (1993); (e) anonymous; (l, m) John Connett, Dec. 1995; (n) Joaquin and Maura Kuhn, *Rats Live* (1981); (o) Jon Agee, *Dynamos* (1994).

72. (a) anonymous; (b) Atlantis, *AP*, Dec. 7, 1901; (c) Willard Espy, *Another Almanac* (1980); (d) O. V. Michaelsen; (e) anonymous; (f) Frans Folks, *GD*, Nov. 28, 1903.

Ecology

73. Smith, Tim S., *TE*, Oct. 1973.

74. John Connett, Nov. 1995.

75. T. H., *AP*, July 1889.

76. (a, b) Atlantis, *TEE*, Apr. 1914.

All Drawn Out

77. (a) El Uqsor, *TE*, Oct. 1956; (b) John Connett, *WWW*, 1995; (c) John Connett, Jan. 1996 in *Palindromist*, Winter 1996.

78. (a) anonymous; (b) Henry Campkin, *N&Q*, Mar. 8, 1873; (c) Leigh Mercer, *N&Q*, Nov. 2, 1946.

79. Dmitri Borgmann, *On Vacation* (1965).

80. Fred Klein, *Palindromist*, winter 1996.

81. Dmitri Borgmann, *On Vacation* (1965).

82. Dmitri Borgmann in Martin Gardner, *O&C* (1961).

Who's There?

83. Jon Agee, *Dynamos* (1994).
84. John Pool, *Daffodil* (1982).
85. (a) Dmitri Borgmann, *On Vacation* (1965); (b) J. A. Lindon in Howard Bergerson, *P&A* (1973).
86. (a) Enavlicm, *TEE*, June 1912; (b) anonymous.

Whodunit?

87. (a, b) Leigh Mercer, *N&Q*, Feb. 1953; (a, b) parentheses, Dmitri Borgmann, *On Vacation* (1965).
88. John Connett, Dec. 1995.
89. (a) Leigh Mercer, *N&Q*, Feb. 1953; (b) Joaquin and Maura Kuhn, *Rats Live* (1981).
90. Dmitri Borgmann in Martin Gardner, *O&C* (1961).
91. Howard Bergerson, *P&A* (1973).
92. J. A. Lindon in Howard Bergerson, *P&A* (1973).
93. Dmitri Borgmann in Martin Gardner, *O&C* (1961).
94. Dmitri Borgmann in Martin Gardner, *O&C* (1961).
95. Dmitri Borgmann in Martin Gardner, *O&C* (1961).
96. Stephen Chism, *From A to Zotamorf* (1992).

Snoops

97. (a) Atlantis, *AP*, Dec. 1, 1907; Enavlicm, *TEE*, June 1912; (b) Ulk, *TE*, May 1994. Both are based on "Was it a rat I saw?" from G. R. Clarke's *Palindromes* (1887).
98. Joaquin and Maura Kuhn, *Rats Live* (1981).
99. anonymous; parentheses, Martin Gardner, *O&C* (1961).
100. (a) Howard Bergerson, *P&A* (1973); (b) anonymous and O. V. Michaelsen; (c) anonymous; (d) G. R. Clarke, *Palindromes* (1887); (e) Henry Campkin, *N&Q*, Mar. 8, 1873

Undone

101. J. A. Lincoln in Howard Bergerson, *P&A* (1973).

102. Jon Agee, *Dynamos* (1994).
103. Jon Agee, *Dynamos* (1994).
104. (a) Carter Bennett, (b) John Connett, *WW*, May 1995.
105. Jon Agee, *Dynamos* (1994).
106. John Pool, *Daffodil* (1982).

Invasion & Evasion

107. Leigh Mercer, *N&Q*, Aug. 30, 1952; "Selim smiles" in
     G. R. Clarke, *Palindromes* (1887).
108. Enavlicm, *TEE*, June 1912.
109. Howard Bergerson, *P&A* (1973).
110. Howard Richler, *WW*, Nov. 1995.
111. John Jensen, "Official Palindrome List," *WWW*,
     April 1995.
113. Jon Agee, *Dynamos* (1994).

Your Money or Your Life

114. and 115. William Camden, *Remains* (1605).
116. Leigh Mercer, *N&Q*, Oct. 16, 1948.
117. Benjamin C. Pearson, *Everyman*, Nov. 28, 1929.
118. G. R. Clarke, *Palindromes* (1887).
119. Joaquin and Maura Kuhn, *Rats Live* (1981).
120. Joaquin and Maura Kuhn, *Rats Live* (1981).
121. Joaquin and Maura Kuhn, *Rats Live* (1981); #107,
     shortened version.
122. Howard Bergerson, *P&A* (1973).
123. (a) Howard Richler, *WW*, May 1993; (b) Leigh Mercer,
     N&Q, July 8, 1950; Mabel P., "Sums are not on Erasmus,"
     Pittsburgh Post, July 8, 1900.
124. Tony Augarde, *Oxford Guide* (1984).

Fleeing Madness

125. (a) anonymous; (b) Joaquin and Maura Kuhn, *Rats Live*
     (1981).

126. (a) Leigh Mercer, *N&Q*, Aug. 30, 1952; (b) G. R. Clarke, *Palindromes* (1887).
127. (a) M. C. S., *Inter-Ocean*, Jan. 31, 1897; (b) Blackstone, *TE*, Oct. 1936.
128. (a) Molemi, *Inter-Ocean*, Mar. 1, 1906; (b) John Connett, May 1996; (c) G. R. Clarke, *Palindromes* (1887).
129. Leigh Mercer, *N&Q*, July 8, 1950.
130. John Connett, July 1996.
131. Hal Ober, *Atlantic Unbound*, Aug. 30, 1996.
132. Jane Prins, *Games*, Apr. 1992.
133. *TE*, June 1956.

Autoshop

134. (a) Tom Deneau; (b) anonymous.
136. J. A. Lindon, *WW*, Nov. 1971.
137. anonymous.
138. Leigh Mercer, *N&Q*, Feb. 1953.

Big Man on Campus

139. (a) *O'London's*, Aug. 31, 1929; (b) anonymous.
140. John Connett, *WWW*, 1995.
141. Leigh Mercer, *N&Q*, Sept. 7, 1946.

Diamonds & Jades, Jacks & Maids

142. M. C. S., *Inter-Ocean*, Jan. 10, 1899.
143. J. A. Lindon in Howard Bergerson, *P&A* (1973).
144. John Connett, Jan. 1996.

Net Results

145. (a) Atlantis, *TEE*, Apr. 1914; (b) Howard Richler, *WW*, May 1992; (c) J. A. Lindon in Howard Bergerson, *P&A* (1973).

Peelings

146. Dmitri Borgmann, *On Vacation* (1965).
147. (a) anonymous; (b) Jouko I. Valta, "International Palindromes" page, *WWW*, Dec. 1995.
148. Smith, Tim S. *TE*, Apr. 1976.
149. Crossman, Jr., in Dr. Crypton, *Science Digest*, Feb. 1983.

"You" Do It

150. El Uqsor, *TE*, 1958.
151. Atlantis, *TEE*, Apr. 1914.
152. Jon Agee, *Go Hang* (1991).
153. Rev. Arthur Pearson, *PP&W* (1908).
154. Dmitri Borgmann, *On Vacation* (1965).
155. John Connett, June 1996.
156. (a) anonymous; (b) Dmitri Borgmann in Martin Gardner, *O&C* (1961).

Politics as Usual

157. J. A. Lindon, *WW*, Nov. 1971.
158. David J. Ray, *San Francisco Chronicle*, 1991.
159. (a, b) Howard Richler, *WW*, Nov. 1991; (c) Mark Saltveit, *Palindromist*, winter 1996; (d) anonymous in Howard Bergerson, *P&A* (1973); (e) Edward Scher in Willard Espy, *Another Almanac* (1980).
160. (a) Enavlicm, *NA*, Sept. 8, 1906; (b) Atlantis, *Inter-Ocean*, 1906: "Star comedy as I say 'Democrats.'"
161. (a) Leigh Mercer, *N&Q*, Sept. 7, 1946; (b) "Name no one(,) man" in Charles Bombaugh, *Gleanings* (1860); (c) Fred J. Abrahams in William Safire, "On Language," *NY Times Magazine*, 1989; (d) Dave Morice, *WW*, Nov. 1996.
162. (a) Dmitri Borgmann, *On Vacation* (1965); (b) Enavlicm, *TEE*, June 1912.
163. Pikmee and Ellen Auriti, *Atlantic Unbound*, Aug. 30, 1996. Political comment about former Republican senator from Kansas Bob Dole.

164. Ron Howes, *Atlantic Unbound*, Aug. 30, 1996.
165. Marg. B., *Atlantic Unbound*, Aug. 30, 1996.

Watergate

166. Smith, Tim S., *TE*, July 1973.
167. Tut, *TE*, Sept. 1973.

Iran-Contra

168. Matthew K. Franklin, *WW*, May 1988.

Panama, 1989

169. Brian Hall "Public Domain Palindrome Page," *WWW*, 1995.
170. (a) David Morice, *WW*, Nov. 1991; (b) *Games*, Apr. 1992.
171. Newrow, *TE*, Mar. 1990.

Persian Gulf War

172. (a) Howard Richler, *WW*, Nov. 1990; "Drat Sadat, a dastard," Michael Miller in Willard Espy, *Another Almanac* (1980); (b) Brian Hall, "Public Domain Palindrome Page," *WWW*, 1995; (c) David Morice, *WW*, May 1992; (d) Howard Richler, *WW*, Nov. 1992.

Bosnia

173. (a) Winfred S. Emmons, *WW*, Feb. 1994; (b) Tom Deneau, *Atlantic Unbound*, Aug. 30, 1996.

Going Places

175. (a) Michael Donner, *I Love Me, vol. I* (1996); (b) Leigh Mercer, *N&Q*, Oct. 16, 1948.
176. Emily P. Arulpragasam, *Atlantic Unbound*, Aug. 30, 1996.
177. Michael Donner, *I Love Me, vol. I* (1996).
178. Emily P. Arulpragasam, *Atlantic Unbound*, Aug. 30, 1996.
179. Peter N. Horne, *Atlantic Unbound*, Aug. 30, 1996.

180. Joaquin and Maura Kuhn, *Rats Live* (1981).
181. (a) without parentheses, Svensk Grandy-bo, *Farmer's Wife*, Aug. 1908; (b) Howard Bergerson, *P&A* (1973).
182. (a) El Uqsor, *TE*, June 1957; (b) Dmitri Borgmann, *On Vacation* (1965).
183. Tom Deneau, *Atlantic Unbound*, Aug. 30, 1996.

Martha, Amy, & Ma

184. Atlantis, *TEE*, Apr. 1914.
185. Jon Agee, *Go Hang* (1991).
186. William Irvine, *If I Had a Hi-Fi* (1992).

About Roses

187. Jim Beloff, *Palindromist*, spring 1997.
188. Howard Bergerson, *P&A* (1973).
189. C. B. Humphrey, *Everyman*, Nov. 28, 1929.
190. (a) Enavlicm, *TEE*, June 1912; (b) parentheses later.

Tan or Hide

191. (a) Smith, Tim S., *TE*, June 1973; (b) Jon Agee, *Go Hang* (1991).

Outerspace

192. Jouko I. Valta, "International Palindromes" page, *WWW*, Dec. 1995.
193. Howard Bergerson, *P&A* (1973).
194. John Connett, *Palindromist*, winter 1996.

Taking Steps

195. Leigh Mercer, *N&Q*, Oct. 16, 1948.
196. George M. Woodcock, *NY Recorder*, Feb. 1893; Woodcock won an award for this contest entry.
197. (a) C. A. H. Greene, *Farmer's Wife*, Aug. 1910; (b) G. R. Clarke, *Palindromes* (1887).

Something Foolish

198. Leigh Mercer, *N&Q*, Oct. 16, 1948.
199. Su San, *TE*, Oct. 1926.
200. *O'London's*, Aug. 31, 1929; parentheses, Leigh Mercer, *N&Q*, Aug. 30, 1952.
202. Atlantis, *TEE*, Apr. 1914.
203. Howard Bergerson, *P&A* (1973).

Oops!

204. (a) anonymous; (b) J. A. Lindon in Howard Bergerson, *P&A* (1973); (c) Jon Agee, *Dynamos* (1994).
205. Martin Gardner, *O&C* (1961).
206. El Uqsor, *TE*, Sept. 1958.
207. (a) Hercules, *TE*, early 1930s; (b) anonymous.

Good & Evil

208. John Connett, Dec. 1995.
209. Howard Bergerson, *P&A* (1973).
210. Dmitri Borgmann, *On Vacation* (1965).
211. (a) anonymous; (b) Philip Morse, *Pittsburgh Post*, Mar. 1900; (c) Mrs. M. K. Barnes, *O'London's*, Dec. 1, 1939.
212. *Everyman*, Nov. 28, 1929.
213. Brian Hall, "Public Domain Palindrome Page," *WWW*, 1995
214. (a) anonymous; (b) Rev. Arthur Pearson, *PP&W* (1908).
215. Cornel G. Ormsby.
216. Howard Bergerson, *P&A* (1973).
217. Anonymous, Tony Augarde, *Oxford Guide* (1984).
218. Howard Bergerson, *P&A* (1973).
219. G. R. Clarke, *Palindromes* (1887).
221. (a) *Everyman*, Nov. 28, 1929; (b) *American N&Q*, Jan. 5, 1889; (c) Dmitri Borgmann in Martin Gardner, *O&C* (1961).
222. Leigh Mercer, *N&Q*, Nov. 2, 1946.
223. Howard Bergerson, *P&A* (1973); "Do good's deeds live never even? Evil's deeds do, O God!" in Rev. Arthur Pearson, *20th Cent. Standard* (1907).

Parting Words

224. J. A. Lindon in Martin Gardner, *O&C* (1961).
225. J. A. Lindon in Martin Gardner, *O&C* (1961).

Chapter 15

More Palindromic Amusements

Cats & Dogs

1. R., *St. Nicholas*, May 1875.
2. King Carnival, *GD*, Oct. 1, 1898.
3. Atlantis, *AP*, Aug. 1, 1905.

Palindromic Names

Famous Names in "Games"

1. Mike Griffin.
2. Susan Leslie and Robert Siegel.
3. David Morice.
5. Susan C. Ridgeway.
6. John Leavy.

Word-Unit Palindromes

James A. Lindon's Collection

1. The first is from *WW*, ca. 1970; the next two were published in Martin Gardner's "Mathematical Games" in *Scientific American* (second, Aug. 1970; third, Sept. 1964); and the last two were in Martin Gardner's *Oddities & Curiosities* (1961).

Index

transposals vs., 73, 89–90
varieties of, 84–90
Anchored reversals, 138
Antigrams (antonymous anagrams, 88–89
Antonyms; *see* Contradictory terms
Aphorisms, 49

B
Baseball
unique player names, 29
Yogi Berra malapropisms, 19
Batman, 24
Berra, Yogi, 19
Bilingual palindrome, 118
Books/literature
famous author names, 32–33
manuscript muses, 16
odd titles, 33
oxymorons, 42–43
shortest English poems, 70
writing advice, 60
Book title abbreviations, 172–174
British broadcast blunders, 25
Businesses' names
as palindromes, 123
unique, 29

C
Carroll, Lewis, 70
Chemical symbols/elements, 62
Chiasmus, 69
City Slickers, 24
Coca-Cola in China, 23
Congress, progress vs., 65
Connected squares, 152
Contradictory terms, 65–68
Contranyms (contronyms), 65–66
pseudo-antonyms, 66–67
pseudo-synonyms, 67–68

stage/screen, 40–41

P

Pairagrams, 86–87
Palindrome dictionaries
   one-word palindromes, 139–143
   reversal dictionary, 128–138
Palindrome examples
   addition, 120
   anchored reversals, 138
   bilingual, 118
   businesses, 123
   cats/dogs, 120
   common proper names, 124
   drop-letter reversals, 138
   earliest palindrome, 116
   famous names, 123–124, 143–144
   foreign-language, 117–119
   most beautiful, 118–119
   musical, 120
   names, 122–123
   owls, 121
   phonetic pals/reversals, 144–145
   poem as, 121
   vertical, 144
   words reconsidered, 146
Palindrome examples (letter-unit), 99–117
   Adam/Eve, 100
   art-related, 106
   autoshop, 110
   big man on campus, 110
   Bosnia, 113
   cigars, 101
   diamonds/jades, Jacks/maids, 110
   drinks all around, 101–102
   ecology, 106
   feeling madness, 109–110
   food, 103–104
   good/evil, 115–116
   invasion/evasion, 108

R

Radio; *see* T.V. and radio
Redividers, 20–21
Reversal dictionary, 128–138
Reversals; *see* Palindrome examples; Palindromes
Reverse parallelisms, 69
Rhymes
   color-related, 11–12
   pelican, 12
   spoonerhymes, 23
   velocity, 12
   word square with, 155–156
Rice, Anne, 29
Riddles
   for female admirers, 14–15
   genealogical, 13–14
   "-gry", 13
Rivers, Joan, 59

S

See-saw tongue-twister, 72
Seven-word squares, 158–162
Short literary works
   Bible verse, 70
   correspondence, 70
   English poems, 70
Silver rhymes, 11–12
Six-word squares, 153–158
Songs
   country, unusual titles, 33
   mishearings of, 20
   oxymorons, 44–46
   proposed titles, 34
Sotadea carmina, 98
Spelling, 61–64; *see also* Words
   chemical symbols/elements, 62
   heteronyms and, 64
   homonyms, homophones, homographs and, 64
   vowels and, 61–62
Spoonerhymes, 23